Love your life - survive the system

A teacher's happiness curriculum

Love your life - survive the system
A teacher's happiness curriculum

© Eilidh Milnes

ISBN 978-1-906316-13-6

Published by Word4Word in 2008.
8 King Charles Court, Evesham, Worcestershire.
www.w4wdp.com

Printed in the UK by Cpod, Trowbridge.

Contents

Foreword

By Chris Roycroft-Davis

We spend the best years of our lives at school, although few pupils realise it at the time. But what about teachers? Can they honestly say that education is as rewarding as they would wish it to be? It should concern us all that many teachers answer that question with a regretful "No", because there are few professions which are as vital to the future of a nation as that of teaching.

We entrust not just the intellectual wellbeing of our children into the hands of these dedicated men and women, but also the social and moral standards that society needs to uphold if civilised behaviour and care for others is to cascade down from generation to generation.

I've spoken to many teachers about the great satisfaction, the spiritual reward, they obtain from seeing young minds and souls bloom and grow under their care. But sadly, I have spoken to many others for whom the classroom is a place of stress, anxiety and unhappiness.

This book has been needed for many years and Eilidh Milnes has done a great service in satisfying that need and presenting her sound advice in such an easy, yet effective, manner. It will give teachers in every area of the profession the inspiration and positive guidance they need to love their lives and be happy.

This book truly reflects the upbeat nature of its author, a woman who will never let a smile or a joyful thought pass her by, and who loves to share her inner strength with others.

But don't think this book is not for you if you're not a teacher. There is learning and nurture here for each and every one of us, whatever vocation we follow. Eilidh has collected many gems of wisdom and a host of stories which richly illustrate that the bright side of life is the place to be – and the place you can be with the right mental attitude.

Treat it as an old friend to whom you can return repeatedly for a fresh dose of common sense and some kind and nourishing words of encouragement and help. That's how I remember some of the great teachers who guided me through school. How I wish

I'd come across a book like this 40 years ago when I was setting out on life's testing adult journey, but thank goodness it's never too late to learn that the purpose of life is a life of purpose.

What greater purpose could there be than planting seeds in young minds that will one day turn into a golden harvest? That task deserves to be rewarding and pleasurable and this book shows how that can be achieved.

Chris Roycroft-Davis, June 2008
http://www.chrisroycroftdavis.com

Preface

When I started to write …*survive the system* I did not know exactly how it would develop and the journey that would ensue. Perhaps being Captain Positive I had an optimistic target to write the book in 90 days. However with the help of my mastermind group, colleagues and clients, friends and family the deadline has been achieved. The difficult part has actually been deciding when to stop. The topic is more complex than I first appreciated. There could be a series of *Love your life…* books to do the subject justice.

During my research Val Webster, a senior educational advisor, asked me a probing question, *"How will you get a balanced viewpoint in your book? How will you know who are truly altruistic professionals and excellent practitioners and those who are 'unique' individuals who are not doing a good job?"*

The answer? I do not know. Many of the book contributions are somewhat subjective. I wanted the content, ideas and offerings to strike a chord with the readers; and at the same time to cause a definite reaction, possibly bringing about a change in thinking or attitude. I must ask you, the reader, to create the balance for yourself. I confess that sometimes I have intentionally included a piece that may prompt a strong emotional response.

I am first and foremost a speaker. A speaker is a storyteller and storytelling is what speakers do best! You enjoy reading or listening to a story, don't you? Good stories well told can bring about changes in behaviour and attitude. Throughout the book I have been flagging options, solutions and ways of managing change. These ideas have been supported and reinforced by stories, poems and anecdotes.

A short story that I loved to tell during my teaching career was entitled *The Hairy Toe*. It was of the Roald Dahl genre. Pupils requested the tale on a regular basis. I would embellish it with gusto and have them on the edge of their seats waiting for the all too familiar punch-line of this eerie ghost-type story.

In my opinion, it is not so much what we read or hear, but the conviction, energy and style with which it is delivered. I trust my passion to help my former profession has come across through my printed words and stories, strategies and action plans. As you move through the chapters I hope you take the opportunity to reflect and move forward in some way.

And remember that you too are a storyteller. There is the opportunity for the talented teacher to pitch as if for a Royal Academy Award during lesson time. Be the star you are. Your students will be happier and respect you all the more.

Have fun!

Dedication

To my gorgeous husband Jay, my personal hero,
and our incredible children Kyle and Catriona, who
have left home to explore the world and have
adventures of their own.

Enjoy!
J.T.
Elledk

What people say
about Eilidh

"Eilidh's workshops have raised staff awareness of simple practical techniques and pro-active systems we can adopt as a school. We find ourselves using her ideas on a daily basis both in our professional lives and at home – especially those with teenagers!

Eilidh's upbeat positivity is a real tonic and just being with her helps us recognise the benefits of seeing the glass 'half full' rather than 'half empty'. We make sure we talk about the good things that are happening in school rather than getting hung up on the difficulties. Eilidh spurs us on to wake up each morning and tell ourselves we are brilliant – what a great way of affirming ourselves and what a wonderful way of raising our childrens' self-esteem."

Carolyn Casserley, Wybunbury Delves CE Aided Primary

"'Inspirational leadership' – the theme of a residential conference for Cheshire primary schools' senior leaders at Shrigley Hall in Macclesfield. Guest speaker was Eilidh Milnes, an internationally acclaimed motivational speaker who explored how to make 'good' teachers 'great' teachers..."

Cheshire County Council

"All of Eilidh's sessions at the Wellbeing Conference were oversubscribed and many head teachers who missed the sessions have received such positive feedback from colleagues that they have requested a return visit.

All evaluation sheets rated Eilidh very highly, not surprising as her sessions delivered meaningful messages in a relaxed and humorous way that was specifically relevant to the delegates. Eilidh's personality is lively and friendly, she is always well prepared, easy to work with and professional in every way."

**Val Cotterill, Chair of Cheshire Association of
Primary head teachers**

"Eilidh,
Yesterday, you spoke to a group of Helsby High School students and my daughter Genevieve was there. She has not stopped talking about you and all the very good advice that you gave to them!"
Maureen Coleman, Head Teacher

"Dear Captain Positive,
The crew of St Nathaniel's CE Primary School returned from your seminar weekend with many happy memories and a renewed sense of purpose. Words used to describe their experiences included: Emotional, Thought Provoking, Enjoyment, Focus, Inspirational, Enlightened, Aspirations, Heart Warming and Strengthening.
   Personally I was impressed by your skills as a speaker. You actively engaged everyone and dealt with individual issues sensitively."
Sharon Sanderson, Head Teacher, Bolton

"I saw your performance today and you really did have an impact on me. (By the way, I'm the girl that is going to become a fashion designer!)
   It was great to see how adults can understand things, because you don't really get much of that. You truly made my day so I would like to thank you."
Krupa, GCSE student at Wellington International School

"Thank you for helping me to help myself..."

Sue Aston, Head teacher

Chapter 1

Introduction

Are you a teacher? Or are you considering entering what, in my opinion, is still one of the finest professions in the world? Are you struggling with your current post, or perhaps a newly qualified teacher (NQT) and full of enthusiasm and energy and in need of encouragement? Are you happy in your position and would really just like help to survive the job and the weight of bureaucracy that has hit the profession in recent years?

Did you enter education thinking it was your vocation, yet seem to have lost your desire or direction? Are you a supply teacher looking for a permanent post? Are you in state education or an independent school? Do you work overseas in an international school? Or are you facing retirement and wondering: what next?

Whatever your situation help is at hand...
I have a passion to help those who work in education. For over a decade, I have been working in schools and colleges in the UK and abroad assisting teachers and lecturers. I have addressed conferences, organised seminars, run workshops, spoken at staff meetings and coached staff one-to-one. I have spoken to teenagers and their parents. And there has been a common feedback message – many teachers need help and support.

Years ago, as an NQT, I was full of fresh ideas and passion. I had always wanted to teach. I was determined to do well, promotion came quickly and I volunteered to attend every course I could get on. I always carried a notebook – my "Good Ideas Book". Little did I realise that this book was to contain survival strategies and become a manual on how to cope in the profession 30 years on.

I would like to say thank you in advance to all my friends, colleagues and delegates whom I have met over the years for their support, fresh ideas and encouragement. You have inspired me to write this book and I hope you find the results beneficial.

What this book provides is some simple practical strategies and skills that you can develop to work for you. I have endeavoured to answer your questions and address your needs and concerns using my personal experience, surveys, latest studies, real life scenarios and, of course, the not so common, common sense.

Before we move on I have a key question:

What do you want to learn about yourself
right now?

Write down two key points:

1. _____

    _____

    _____

    _____

    _____

    _____

    _____

    _____

2. _____

    _____

    _____

    _____

    _____

    _____

    _____

    _____

How to get the most out of this book

Many people find it hard to write in a book or to highlight sections but this book is a tool to be used. And like most tools it is useless unless you take it out of the packaging and start to use it. I am well aware of how much of your time is spent reading, marking and preparing for lessons. So, it is vital that you use your personal reading time effectively.

Here are some tips to help you – a time challenged teacher – get maximum results:

1. Use *Love your life - survive the system* as a workbook for your notes and ideas. It will chart your progress. At a glance you will be able to see how well you have applied the success strategies which are relevant to you. The book is printed in a format that is ideal for highlighting your action points.

2. Review your notes on a weekly/monthly basis. Use the book as a tool to solve your daily problems.

3. Use highlighter pens as you read and mark the parts that strike you as important with a light bulb or ☺symbol. This will make re-reading so much quicker and more effective. Select a colour such as red to highlight priority tasks.

4. Double underscore ideas that are a major priority to you.

5. Decide today to make the necessary changes to gain a work/life balance and improve relationships in your life. Develop a desire to get the most out of your life and out of this book.

6. As you read, if an idea has resonance for you, stop and say to yourself: How can I apply that to my life? Will that suggestion work for me? Perhaps it has more relevance to colleagues, if so note it down to share at the next staff meeting.

7. Suggest to colleagues that you take an aspect of the book and use it as a personal development topic at your next inset training day – use the free PDF downloads available on my website to assist you.

When to use this book

Create a regular reading for pleasure habit.
Make it a routine – ten minutes a day is a good way to start.

Benefits to you and your organisation

By the end of the book you should:

- Understand the importance of achieving a work/life balance that suits you, your lifestyle and your teaching role

- Identify the benefits of achieving an effective balanced lifestyle

- Identify ways to improve and maintain satisfactory time management

- Be able to set clear goals around your own life priorities. This will lead to increased morale in your education establishment, job satisfaction and a more balanced life.

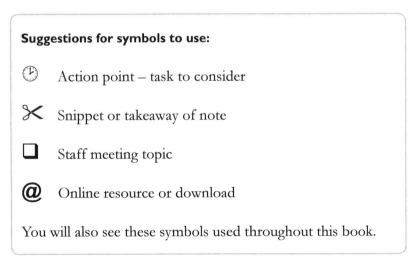

Suggestions for symbols to use:

🕐   Action point – task to consider

✂   Snippet or takeaway of note

❑   Staff meeting topic

@   Online resource or download

You will also see these symbols used throughout this book.

To download the free PDF files visit www.eilidhmilnes.com, register as a member and download the files you require entering member code 'LYLmemg88'.

Sign up to the blog: http://loveyourlife-eilidh.blogspot.com

Notes: _____

Work like you don't need the money

Dance like no one is watching

Sing like no one is listening

Love like you've never been hurt

And live life every day as if it were your last

An anonymous quotation or,
according to some sources, an old Irish proverb.
(Either way the words are well worth pondering.)

Chapter 2

Why teach?

Why did you become a teacher? Or why are you considering doing so now? What made you choose this profession above others? Is it a vocation or just a convenient income? Take a few moments to reflect. Perhaps write down your reasons and weigh up your responses.

As a teacher you are a leader in your community and in your family. How will you pass along the knowledge and the lessons you have learned? How will you share the experiences of your journey to where you are today? Will you write them, record them, discuss, or demonstrate them? There is no one right way to impart knowledge. The important thing is to communicate and allow your understanding to connect with those whose lives you touch. You have an opportunity to be a hero (or heroine) and with that comes responsibilities. You can connect with others and allow them to learn, think, debate, grow, change and prosper. You can be a person of influence. This was certainly one of the main drivers in my joining the profession years ago and still applies today in my speaking and coaching career.

Why *are* you still here?

Are you still fired up by your career choice? We all work for money, however it is seldom rewarding if it is the only motivating factor. How do you feel about these words: *"Work like you don't need the money. Dance like no one is watching. Sing like no one is listening. Love like you've never been hurt. And live life every day as if it were your last"*? I first read this quotation when I visited the Eden Project in Cornwall. I copied the words and printed out the powerful quote. When I need inspiration I read it and it warms my heart.

Another quotation that strikes a chord with me is: "You can only become truly accomplished at something you love. Don't make money your goal. Instead, pursue the things you love doing, and then do them so well that people can't take their eyes off you." (Maya Angelou, American poet). In fact this quotation had such an impact on me that I often use it after my signature. What do you do to keep alive your excitement and enthusiasm for the job?

T + S + R = HT
The formula for Happy Teachers

I joined the profession in the '70s not knowing what my monthly salary was going to be; when I received my first pay-cheque I thought I was really well off. That may sound naïve today, yet it is true. Imagine it! I was being paid for something I loved and would almost have done for free! It took me some time to appreciate society's salary status and perceptions related to incomes, yet on the whole these matters did not concern me because I had a passion for my job and I felt it a worthy career.

T + S + R = HT is my happy teacher formula. It translates to

T+ - teacher plus

S+ - salary (adequate) plus

R = - respect equals

HT - happy teachers

I suspect that when teachers considered going on strike this year for the first time in over two decades, it was less to do with money and more to do with the lack of respect for the profession that pervades society nowadays.

What do you do to keep alive your excitement, commitment and enthusiasm for the job when faced with such circumstances? For example, do you identify with the three quotes below?

Words Work Well (WWW)

I have spoken to thousands of teachers over the years and have actively sought out their opinions. Here are some of their words – cameos that may have resonance with you:

"I love teaching... and even in my darkest hour I could not imagine leaving the profession..." Carolyn Casserley (Head Teacher)

"Teaching drives me crazy at times, but I cannot imagine doing anything else..." Jacqui Ratcliffe (Principal Teacher)

"Great teachers know that they are always on stage. They know who they are, how they act, and what they believe in. This is as important as what they teach..." Gary Edwards (Head of Sixth Form)

In my leadership sessions, I encourage teachers to move from a position of being good to that of being great. In my opinion, great teachers give us a sense not only of who they are but, more importantly, of who we are and who we might become. They unlock our energies, imaginations and minds. They are vital and full of passion. Effective teachers pose compelling questions, explain options, teach us to reason, suggest possible directions and urge us on. The best teachers, like the best leaders, have an uncanny ability to step outside themselves and become liberating forces in our lives.

What is your idea of a great teacher? Are not teachers the greatest resource in education? In your opinion, who is a great teacher?

Good to great

As Jim Collins (business consultant, author and lecturer) says: "Turning good into great takes energy, but the building of momentum adds more energy back into the pool than it takes out. Conversely, perpetuating mediocrity is an inherently depressing process and drains far more energy out of the pool than it puts back in."

Mediocrity be damned! Let's all aim to go from good to great!

To quote Jim Collins again: "People are not the most important asset – the *right* people are." And for me proof of this is working with school staff.

For example, head teacher Anne Doughton booked me to speak to her staff on the topic of stress awareness at Mollington Banastre Hotel. The location and setting were perfect and that in itself created the right atmosphere and tone for the event. I think it essential that teachers have training sessions off-site, especially when the topics are in the well being, self esteem and stress awareness arena. A quality environment will create the correct mindset and makes staff feel valued.

Anne and her deputy Jonathan Melville may not have read Jim Collins' work, however they did realise the importance of getting the right staff. It must have been reassuring for them to have confirmation of this knowledge during our training day.

Part of the programme was based on a simple profiling technique, which proved to be illuminating and a lot of fun. The most normal and ordinary thing is for us to see the world from our own perspective; the most extraordinary thing is to see life from the perspective of others. And that is what we explored that day.

Every behaviour style has strengths and weaknesses. We identified strengths, worked on weaknesses, discovered some motivational secrets, raised the general feeling of self-confidence and awareness and developed a great team spirit. And we focused on going from being good to great.

To paraphrase Jim Collins, I am not suggesting that going from good to great is easy, or that every organisation will successfully make the shift. By definition, it is not possible for everyone to be above average. But I am suggesting that those who strive to turn good into great find the process no more painful or exhausting than those who settle for average.

Another feature of a great teacher is the ability to overcome and keep on keeping on when the going gets tough. The interview below is an example of this:

Interview with Nance

Nance is a primary teacher who is single and has no children. She taught year six for 11 years, was an assistant head for one year and she is currently teaching year one.

Q. What is the most difficult situation you have had to deal with in your teaching career?

Dealing with the sudden death of my Mum while the school was in very challenging circumstances in every area.

Q. Can you please outline the circumstances?

The school had recently amalgamated. There was also a new build. It was a school causing concern, was part of the Integrated Services Programme (ISP) and had a new head. It was in an area of high social deprivation with all the extra challenges this brings.

Q. How did you deal with these very hard times?

I continued after the death of my Mum for one year and then decided that I needed to take some valuable time out for my sanity and to support my Dad. I resigned and sold my house, using the equity to support myself. I then spent irreplaceable time with my family, took a couple of holidays and reassessed what was important to me. I then began to put back into my life what was important to me!

Q. Who helped you?

Colleagues reassured me that it would be a valuable experience and my family supported me as ever.

Q. What assistance/support did you get from the education authority/your head teacher?

Not applicable really. Although to be fair the head was supportive but the decision was completely my own.

Q. What worked and what didn't?

It just worked! I have a renewed outlook and constantly remind myself of what is truly important.

Q. What have you learned from these experiences?

I have figured out the hard way what matters the most to me and also what I can live without.

Q. How can others benefit from your experience?

Remember that when you feel like you can least afford a break (financially, emotionally or from a work perspective) that's exactly when you should take one. Take the risk. Ask yourself: What's the worst that can happen? And, more importantly: What's the best that can happen?

Q. Can you list your key success strategies for dealing with future issues (things to share with others in similar circumstances)?

1. Take a break when you least feel like you should.

2. Remind yourself regularly that you only have one life.

3. Have the courage to say something has to change – and then change it!!

I believe this to be excellent advice. Perhaps we should also remember this quotation by Annie Dillard (writer and poet): "How we spend our days is, of course, how we spend our lives."

Nance was prepared to take a risk to achieve a better and more balanced life. Do you think it worked for her? Do you need to take a few risks in order to see a better outcome in your life? Is it time to pause, reflect and make a few more notes?

Interview with PD

PD is a single, female teacher, who worked full time as a classroom teacher for 33 years. She took early retirement at 55. She currently does some supply teaching and a little private tutoring.

Q. What is the most difficult situation you have had to deal with in your teaching career?

Ofsted! The concept and how it is perceived, not the actual inspectors. I can remember HM inspections - and the frequency of Ofsted visits today is inappropriate.

Q. Can you please outline the circumstances?

Ofsted makes you begin to question your own abilities. The prospect of Ofsted drives some people to breaking point. We know that they can't take us out and shoot us but it does feel that way for some folks.

Q. How did you deal with these very hard times?

Well you try to be perfect and that in its turn causes more strain. Good teachers take a pride in their work and they fear that they will be slated. Ofsted is not there for teachers.

Q. Who helped you?

The quality of colleagues is vital. Members of staff have to get on and support each other. We have to keep a close eye on team members and spot if anyone is going down and do things to cheer them. I've been known to say: "Hang on a minute, let's come back down to earth and look at this realistically!"

Q. What assistance/support did you get from the education authority/your head teacher?

Mutual support was the greatest help.

Q. What have you learned from these experiences?

Be willing to talk to colleagues and friends about things. Perhaps find a mentor or coach. Do not depend on the system to support you.

Q. Can you list your key success strategies for dealing with future issues (things to share with others in similar circumstances)?

1. Some years ago, I found a little book on list building and it has been most helpful. Invaluable in fact. It is called *100 Essential Lists for Teachers* (see Eilidh's booklist **@**).

2. I have used the concepts in the book and adapted them to my life in retirement.

3. Learn to gradually adapt to retirement and perhaps do part-time or voluntary work to bridge the gap. Find different and challenging things to do.

4. Do not feel guilty. I was born to a generation that worked and expected to contribute to society. I loved teaching. It was my vocation. I felt guilty that I was no longer doing my bit. I am so glad that I was asked back to my former school to do supply work. I feel this way that I am still worthy and able to help.

PD stated that Ofsted was the most difficult situation she had to deal with in her 33-year teaching career. How does that make you feel?

Sadly, facts prove that she is not alone. PD said that it was vital to support each other under times of stress and crisis and it is apparent that many teachers see Ofsted as a potential disaster situation. Such guidance was not enough for two members of the profession who found that an Ofsted Inspection was sufficient to drive them to committing suicide.

I refer to two cases; that of Keith Waller, who was an experienced teacher at a primary school and highly regarded by colleagues, pupils and parents. He was a popular teacher who killed himself after complaining of being victimised and bullied at the school where he worked. And secondly, to the case of head teacher Irene Hogg who led a school in Scotland. Like PD, she had been a teacher for 33 years and had been considering taking early retirement. The inspectors criticised her school, she feared the results and this drove her to take her own life. What tragedies!

Where are the support systems, the counsellors, advisors and unions in such cases? These are extreme examples but many teachers will identify with the feelings of panic and fear. Most of us know teachers whose health has been affected by Ofsted inspections. There is a huge pressure on staff during inspections and someone has to take that pressure off before the matter gets out of hand.

Have you lost your Why?

Have you lost sight of your reasons for joining the teaching profession?

Here are three thought provoking questions:

1. **What would you do if you were made redundant?**

2. **What would you do if you were given six months to live?**

3. **If you won the lottery tomorrow, what would you do?**

And three practical steps to take while you contemplate your future:

1. **Update your CV – at least every six months. You could create your own web-page for self-promotion.**

2. **Network and develop contacts both within and outside of education. Tell people what you want and ask them for help.**

3. **Talk to people you respect and admire. Ask them for an honest appraisal of your skills and abilities. Act on their suggestions if you feel them valid.**

Time to move on?

If after due diligence and deliberation you seem to hate all kids and not just the difficult ones, your heart sinks on the first day of term, and you are reluctant to admit to being a teacher, then maybe it is time to go.

Remember that teachers can and do make the transition into alternative employment. You are well suited to apply for positions in training, consultancy, counselling and publishing for example. You have many skills; all you need to do is identify them. But bear in mind all the benefits of teaching such as the precious school holidays – particularly appealing to teachers with young families.

Take a sheet of A4. Divide it into two columns headed Pros and Cons and then list all the good and bad things about your current position; then discuss the results with someone you respect to give you an impartial hearing.

Promotion, exchange or overseas posting

Maybe all you need is a sabbatical. Or perhaps you need to look at career options in a different school? Could you take a career break abroad for example and teach overseas? There are many worldwide organisations and all you have to do is Google "teaching abroad" and check out the options.

One I can recommend is **http://www.gemseducation.com**. GEMS is a group of international schools and as it expands its ever-growing network into a vast number of countries, opportunities will arise for employment and new positions will become available. On the other hand you could research the option of a teacher exchange, a straightforward job swap. I know of several friends who took this option. Teacher exchange information can be found on **http://www.tes.co.uk**.

You may also want to read the interview at: **http://news. uk.msn.com/teacher-strike-q-and-a.aspx** entitled the Tale of Two Teachers. It covers the views of two teachers who switched life in London classrooms for those in foreign countries and considers what it is really like to live on a teacher's salary in the UK.

Another option could be to be involved in a Comenius programme. Comenius projects cover pre-schools through to upper secondary schools. The Comenius programme seeks to develop understanding of and between various European cultures through exchanges and co-operation between schools in different countries – these experiences foster personal development, skills and competences, and cultivate the notion of European citizenship (**http://ec.europa.eu/education/programmes/llp/ comenius/index_en.html**).

Getting on and getting out

If you come to the conclusion that it is time to move on then I urge you to leave a first class impression behind you. Work hard right up until the end. This will keep you in the right frame of mind to start afresh and keep your good reputation intact. Keep close counsel and share the news of your departure with sensitivity. Others may have very mixed feelings about the resignation of a colleague. Regardless of how you feel about your boss and colleagues never lambast them in public. Always look to find the good, thank everyone for helping and supporting you. This can only help you especially if you are going to be looking for testimonials in the future.

Project manage your leaving. Liaise with your replacement and leave everything in good order. Remember the children will need you right up until the end so do the best you can. If you have a leaving party then do stay sober, keep your leaving speech short, say only positive things and leave ahead of the crowd. You may feel sad, have doubts and regret your decision at the end. However, this is only natural as one chapter of your life closes. Make the effort to focus on your future as you walk out of the staffroom for the last time and think of all the positive changes that are about to take place.

Notes:

Story time

As she stood in front of her class on the very first day of school, Mrs Thompson told the children an untruth. Like most teachers, she looked at her students and said that she loved them all the same. However, that was impossible, because there in the front row, slumped in his seat, was a little boy named Teddy Stoddard.

Mrs Thompson had watched Teddy the year before and noticed that he did not play well with the other children, that his clothes were messy and that he constantly needed a bath. In addition, Teddy could be unpleasant. It got to the point where Mrs Thompson would actually take delight in marking his papers with a broad red pen, making bold Xs and then putting a big 'F' at the top of his papers.

At the school where Mrs Thompson taught, she was required to review each child's past records and she put Teddy's off until last. However, when she reviewed his file, she was in for a surprise.

Teddy's first teacher wrote: "Teddy is a bright child with a ready laugh. He does his work neatly and has good manners... he is a joy to be around."

His second teacher wrote: "Teddy is an excellent student, well liked by his classmates, but he is troubled because his mother has a terminal illness and life at home must be a struggle."

His third teacher wrote: "His mother's death has been hard on him. He tries to do his best, but his father doesn't show much interest, and his home life will soon affect him if some steps aren't taken."

Teddy's next teacher wrote: "Teddy is withdrawn and doesn't show much interest in school. He doesn't have many friends and he sometimes sleeps in class."

By now, Mrs Thompson realised the problem and she was ashamed of herself. She felt even worse when her students brought her Christmas presents, wrapped in beautiful ribbons and bright paper, except for Teddy's. His present was clumsily wrapped in the heavy, brown paper that he got from a grocery bag. Mrs Thompson took pains to open it in the middle of the other presents. Some of the children started to laugh when she found a rhinestone bracelet with some of the stones missing, and a bottle that was one-quarter full of perfume. But she stifled the children's laughter when she exclaimed how pretty the bracelet was, putting it on, and dabbing some of the perfume on her wrist. Teddy Stoddard stayed after school that day just long enough to say, 'Mrs Thompson, today you smelled just like my Mum used to.'

After the children left, she cried for at least an hour. On that very day she quit teaching reading, writing and arithmetic. Instead, she began to teach children. Mrs Thompson paid particular attention to Teddy. As she worked with him, his mind seemed to come alive. The more she encouraged him, the faster he responded. By the end of the year, Teddy had become one of the smartest children in the class and, despite her lie that she would love all the children the same, Teddy became one of her "teacher's pets". And all the children seemed to flourish.

A year later, she found a note under her door, from Teddy, telling her that she was the best teacher he ever had in his whole life. Six years went by before she got another note from Teddy. He then wrote that he had finished high school, third in his class, and she was still the best teacher he had ever had in his life. Four years after that she got another letter, saying that while things had been tough at times, he'd stayed in school, had stuck with it, and would soon graduate from college with the highest of honours. He assured Mrs Thompson that she was still the best and favourite teacher he had ever had in his whole life.

Four years later and yet another letter came. This time he explained that after he got his bachelor's degree, he decided to go a little further. The letter explained that she was still the best and favourite teacher he ever had. But now his name was a little longer – the letter was signed, Theodore F Stoddard, MD.

The story does not end there. You see, there was yet another letter that spring. Teddy said he had met this girl and was going to be married. He explained that his father had died a couple of years ago and he was wondering if Mrs Thompson might agree to sit at the wedding in the place that was usually reserved for the mother of the groom. Of course, Mrs Thompson did. And guess what? She wore that bracelet, the one with several rhinestones missing. Moreover, she made sure she was wearing the perfume that Teddy remembered his mother wearing on their last Christmas together.

They hugged each other, and Dr Stoddard whispered in Mrs Thompson's ear: "Thank you Mrs Thompson for believing in me. Thank you so much for making me feel important and showing me that I could make a difference."

Mrs Thompson, with tears in her eyes, whispered back: "Teddy, you have it all wrong. You were the one who taught me that I could make a difference. I didn't know how to teach until I met you."

Don't quit

When things go wrong, as they sometimes will,

When the road you're trudging seems all uphill,

When the funds are low the debts are high,

And you want to smile, but you have to sigh,

When care is pressing you down a bit,

Rest, if you must – but don't you quit.

Life is queer with it's twists and turns,

As everyone of us sometimes learns,

And many a failure turns about

When he might have won had he stuck it out.

Don't give up, though the pace seems slow –

You may succeed with another blow,

Often the struggler has given up

When he might have captured the victor's cup.

And he learned too late, when the night

slipped down,

How close he was to the golden crown.

Success is failure turned inside out –

The silver tint of the clouds of doubt –

And you never can tell how close you are,

It may be near when it seems afar;

So stick to the fight when you're hardest hit –

It's when things seem worst that you mustn't quit!

Anonymous

A final plea just before you go

So, with the above story and poem in mind and before you go off to consider another career, can I make a closing appeal for my beloved and often beleaguered profession?

Where will you find the same challenges, sense of purpose, sense of self-worth, prestige, responsibility, team spirit, excitement and joy in the satisfaction of a job well done?

Where else but in teaching do you get the opportunity to be a hero in the lives of young people, to set a good example, to influence young minds and the opportunity to contribute to society?

I rest my case.

Notes: _____

_____

_____

_____

_____

_____

_____

_____

_____

_____

_____

_____

_____

_____

_____

_____

_____

Be a good
finder

Chapter 3

Strategies for coping with stress

The causes of stress

By 2020, the World Health Organisation predicts that depression and stress related illnesses will be the second biggest health issue next to heart disease. In western society, we are willing slaves to work and many of us struggle to find balance and peace of mind. And if stress in the workplace is not enough, emotional distress has also reached epidemic proportions.

According to the National Union of Teachers (NUT) research, *Tackling Stress in Teachers*, published in 1999 and 2007, a wide range of factors are responsible:

- Excessive workload and working hours

- Rising class sizes

- Pressures from Ofsted inspections

- Changes in courses, curriculum and testing requirements

- Poor management and workplace bullying

- Pupil misbehaviour, risk of violence from pupils, parents and intruders

- Lack of support from bureaucracy, form filling and routine tasks

- Lack of job security due to redundancy, fixed term contracts and school closures

- Lack of control over the job, burden of providing cover and threat to early retirement arrangement

- Denigration of profession by politicians and media and the lack of public esteem.

In support of these findings, another research document, this time released by Durham University in November 2006, found that the issues of workload and pupil behaviour were the most important factors in dissuading teachers from entering the profession or possibly causing them to leave.

Not surprisingly, these findings are also mirrored in a survey that I carried out in November 2007 at a conference for senior leaders in education in Cheshire. Over 100 delegates attended and 77 volunteered to respond. Here are a selection of comments:

Diane Woolrid:
"There are too many initiatives and SATs linked to league tables."

Joyce Evers:
"Because there are so many initiatives, there are too many things to do – and not enough time to be with the children individually."

Helen Maxwell:
"There is so much negativity from the government, the newspapers and the media. The goal posts are always changing and we cannot get supply cover!"

Angela Birkenshaw:
"There is so much paperwork it is hard to keep it all in perspective. It is important to be well organised and use time wisely, however the paperwork and marking make it very difficult."

It follows then that a great number of teachers are under pressure and therefore stressed; and while there is a tremendous need to create working environments that are stimulating and challenging it is also essential that they are rewarding and balanced.

Consider Sheila's responses to the survey questions. She is a female teacher in the 40-50 age range. As you read her comments, note how you would have answered the questions:

Q1A *On average, how many hours do you physically spend in the school building each day?*

Answer: Nine

Your answer: _____

Q1B *On average, how much extra time do you spend working at home each day?*

Answer: Two hours

Your answer: _____

Q2 *If you could change one thing about teaching today, what would it be?*

Answer: Less paperwork

Your answer: _____

Q3 *Can you share a stress prevention tip with colleagues who are finding it hard to maintain a work/life balance?*

Answer: Take up a hobby and don't use work as an excuse to miss it. I've taken up dancing and love it.

Your answer: _____

Q4 *What is the number one cause of stress in your working life?*

Answer: Too much to do!

Your answer: _____

Q5 *Any other comments/advice/observations you wish to add?*

Answer: I love teaching. More teaching assistant support for less able children would be welcomed.

Your answer: _____

How do your answers compare with Sheila's?

Strategies

The world is full of strategies to help you deal with stress and work/life balance. You're supposed to slow down, take more exercise and meditate; you're supposed to eat fibre for breakfast and fresh fish for dinner and drink eight glasses of water a day; and don't forget that all important task of list making. But do you really need to make another attempt at living a balanced life? Or does this just add to your stress levels? Is it empty rhetoric or does it really work?

Many teachers are on sick leave due to stress. They talk about experiencing huge feelings of guilt due to the fact that they have been off for several weeks. Mike, a year head, told me recently: "If I had broken my arm or had any physical illness, I think it would have been easier to handle. If I had something that was visible, it would be different. The trouble is there are still so many people out there who don't understand depression or stress-related problems, and think it's a case of 'pull yourself together and carry on'."

He added: "I think I have brought on my own stress by taking everything too seriously. I originally trained as a primary teacher and transferred into secondary. The trouble is I completely underestimated the amount of crowd control needed for the job, and especially with the larrikins in an inner city school where the lack of discipline is madness. I fear for my sanity!"

Another case in point is Jane, a nursery teacher. She is very conscientious and dedicated to her job. In fact, she seems to think and plan for her work 24/7. Sadly, one of the casualties of her commitment has been her marriage. She divorced after eight years. The amount of time Jane allocated to her career undoubtedly played a factor in the deterioration of her personal relationship. A year after this personal upheaval, Jane's school had a visit from Ofsted. Rightly or wrongly they graded Jane as satisfactory. After all her devotion and near fanaticism this was an insult – the final blow to her mental anguish that led to a complete breakdown. In her eyes the grading was unacceptable. To seek redress seemed pointless and Jane rapidly went into a downward spiral that culminated in her being off work with stress for a term. It has been a long hard and on-going battle for her to get back on track, and even today Jane has setbacks and black days. She still has time off due to stress. She still takes a daily anti-depressant.

Jane and Mike are not unique. Their stories will be all too familiar to you I am sure.

Story time

A lecturer, when explaining stress management to an audience, raised a glass of water and asked: "How heavy is this glass of water?" The answers ranged from 20g to 500g.

"The absolute weight," said the lecturer, "doesn't matter. It depends on how long you try to hold it. If I hold it for a minute, that's not a problem. If I hold it for an hour, I'll have an ache in my right arm. If I hold it for a day, you'll have to call an ambulance!

"In each case, it's the same weight, but the longer I hold it, the heavier it becomes. And that's the way it is with stress. If we carry our burdens all the time, sooner or later, as the burden becomes increasingly heavy, we won't be able to carry on. As with the glass of water, you have to put it down for a while and rest before holding it again. When we're refreshed, we can carry on with the burden.

"So it is with our jobs," he added. "Before you return home tonight, put the burden of work down. Don't carry it home. You can pick it up tomorrow. Whatever burdens you're carrying now, let them down for a moment if you can. Relax; pick them up later after you've rested."

Dwell on this quotation for a moment:

"There never seems enough time to do it right, but there always seems to be enough time to do it over." *Anonymous.*

How often do you feel under pressure to meet targets and time constraints? Do you find yourself wishing that you had time to do your job 'properly'; do you think that your school, boss, team or colleagues could be more supportive? Your personal wellbeing and the success of your organisation depend upon the proper and effective use of time, and the way you react to pressure.

Today about 50 per cent of women in the Western world work; in the UK, one in five families is headed by a solo woman as against one in 50 headed by a solo man. When we consider the gender facts it is frightening especially when so many teachers (in primary in particular) are women. While both men and women have it tough in the workplace, these statistics highlight the plight of a large proportion of female teachers in the UK.

Notes: _____

_____

_____

_____

_____

_____

_____

_____

_____

_____

_____

_____

_____

_____

_____

_____

_____

Work/Life balance

"Life is like riding a bike. It is impossible to maintain your balance while standing still." *Linda Brakeall (Ex-teacher, now author and businesswoman)*

Joy, a recently retired head teacher of a primary school in Cheshire, should give you inspiration. "I do feel though that stress is a result of poor organisation both personal and institutional, with the institutional being the main component. As a head, I was very keen to develop a strong team spirit where everyone was aware of school issues and felt involved in decision making. Mutual support and respect were expected and everyone shared a joint responsibility for behaviour for every child, not just their own class. This meant children felt secure and behaviour (which can be a major stress issue) was always being monitored.

"To maintain team spirit we often did things together and one Inset day was always set aside for fun! We did things from walking in the hills to flying to Amsterdam (to look at the art, of course). Much stress is inflicted by external agencies and as a head I felt it was important to only do those things that would be helpful to us and not jump in with both feet when new initiatives were introduced. For example, we were a high achieving English school so did not incorporate all the literacy strategy when it was introduced. We included only bits that might improve us further and lots of long useless staff meetings were avoided."

Why not have your staff meeting in Dublin or Amsterdam? What a great opportunity to team build and have shared experiences. Would you feel special and worthy if your next staff training day was in Paris? If not, why not?

What I do find amazing is that people do the same things over and over again and yet expect different results. How bizarre is that? To get different results you need to see and do things differently… and go to places you have never been!

My speaking and coaching services have been developed in response to a tremendous need to create working environments that are stimulating, rewarding and balanced. Many of these are relevant to schools and I have tailored them accordingly.

Here are some common sense ideas that can make a big difference:

1. List your personal commitments in order of importance, eg family, extended family, friends, relaxation, hobbies or leisure activities.

2. Break down your working day into categories such as business or topic development, internal meetings, seminars and so on. Make a comprehensive list.

3. Allocate time to each activity in point 2 (include weekends).

4. Look at the big picture. Regardless of whether you think you have any choice, are you devoting too much time to work at the expense of your personal life? If you are and this is causing you anxiety, it's time to act. Think about what your ideal work/life balance would be.

5. Look for a mentor/business friend/coach for input.

6. Set realistic goals. If you currently work 12-hour days, it's unlikely you'll be able to change to an eight-hour day straightaway. However, improved time-management can enable you to finish earlier.

7. Reward yourself every time you make progress.

8. Be selfish with every second. Stop doing things that are a waste of your time. Rationalise. Use your time to the maximum benefit.

9. Improve your habits. We all make to-do lists... Now create stop lists, ie stop checking email every hour – check it at 9am and 5pm only. Stop watching so much television. Stop drinking that extra glass of alcohol. Stop forwarding unnecessary emails. Stop unnecessary meetings. Stop the pity parties.

10. Delegate tasks to others – learn to let go. Consider outsourcing some of your management activities to external suppliers such as a freelance book-keeper or bursar.

11. Take regular breaks. Removing yourself from the location for some fresh air will make you less stressed, more focused and productive.

Story time

Two young boys were raised by an alcoholic father. As they grew older, they moved away from their broken home, each going their own way in the world. Several years later, they happened to be interviewed separately by a psychologist, who studied the effects of drunkenness on children in broken homes. His research revealed that the two men were strikingly different from each other. One was a clean-living teetotaller; the other, a hopeless drunk like his father.

The psychologist asked each of them why he developed the way he did, and each gave an identical answer: "What else would you expect, when you have a father like mine?"

This story was revealed by Dr Hans Selye, an internationally renowned Canadian physician and scientist known as 'the father of stress'. A medical pioneer, he devoted the majority of his years to the exploration of biological stress. The story demonstrates a cardinal rule implicit in stress, health and human behaviour.

Use your
stop list

Reactions to stress

According to RH Schuller, a writer in the realm of positive thinking: "It is not what happens to you in life that makes the difference. It is how you react to each circumstance you encountered that determines the result. Every human being in the same situation has the possibilities of choosing how he will react – either positively or negatively."

Thus, stress is not necessarily caused by stressor agents; rather, it is caused by the way stressor agents are perceived, interpreted, or appraised in each individual case. Outside events and people upset some more than others, because they are looked upon and dealt with in entirely different ways. The stressors may even be the same in each case, yet the reaction will almost always be different in different people.

Armed with that kind of information, it would seem that we can greatly improve our reactions to stressful situations. What seems to be a cruel world to one person might be filled with challenge and opportunity to another. It is our reaction that makes the difference.

Dr Maxwell Maltz, an American cosmetic surgeon and author, is a firm believer in negative thinking when used correctly.

"We need to be aware of negatives so that we can steer clear of them. A golfer needs to know where the bunkers and sand traps are – but he doesn't think continuously about the bunker – where he doesn't want to go. His mind 'glances' at the bunker, but he dwells upon the green."

So, you need to know what is causing negativity in your life, acknowledge it and then steer away from the destructive influences of thinking negative thoughts.

I shared my conclusion with a teacher I like and respect. This was her feedback (or feed forward as I like to call it): "I can think of a lot more. Not treating children as a statistic. Not thinking that learning is a set of stairs that only goes in one direction – up! Not requiring a 'prediction' at five of what a child's results will be at 11 and penalise teachers when they don't make it... (don't start me off!!) You don't need a rant from me at this stage."

Although these comments seem negative, I am sure readers will see how they can bring about positive change in a failing system.

Interview with Elaine Hanzak

Elaine spent almost 20 years as a teacher for children of all ages, with severe and profound learning difficulties. Originally it was her passion, but in her words: "Over the years the pointless paperwork and poor management killed the enthusiasm I once had for it."

She is now a full-time speaker on mental health issues, specifically around childbearing, based on the book of her experiences: *Eyes without sparkle – a journey through postnatal illness.* Elaine is married with one son and based in Cheshire, UK. Her website is **www.elainehanzak.co.uk**.

Q. What is the most difficult situation you have had to deal with in your teaching career?

Within a six-month period three of my pupils out of the nine in the class, died from different causes.

Q. Can you please outline the circumstances?

After I had been off for an extended maternity and sick leave due to developing puerperal psychosis, I finally was well enough to return to teaching. I was put in a class for the children with profound and complex learning difficulties. Many of the pupils were tube fed and had many medical needs.

I had to manage my grieving team of assistants, grieving pupils (none of whom could vocalise) and be a support to the families. The attitude from management appeared to be purely concerned over falling numbers.

Q. How did you deal with these very hard times?

Talking to my immediate staff and researching the best ways to help the remaining pupils cope with the loss of their peers did help. We ensured that for the children still in our class everyday would be happy and fulfilled, with fun at the top of the agenda.

Q. Who helped you?

My teaching assistants and a student who was on placement with us.

Q. What assistance/support did you get from the education authority/your head teacher?

Very little. The following year we had a new school nurse – she offered support then but our regret was that she had not been with us in our time of need.

Q. What worked and what didn't?

We made memory books and boards about the children who had died and would talk about them and happy memories in the day-to-day running of the class.

Q. What have you learned from these experiences?

It felt like the heart and caring side had been lost in the teaching profession. It seemed like we just had to get on with the teaching tasks. The national curriculum also seemed pointless for these children. I remember having a parent review for a teenage boy who was very severely physically and mentally disabled. He had no verbal communication and was completely dependent for all his needs. Yet I had to tell his parents about which Shakespeare play we had been studying and what our theme in French was! They looked at me like I was completely mad!

I learned that I had to find my own survival techniques. I resigned when I had the opportunity to become a speaker.

Q. How can others benefit from your experience?

- Do not let the profession make you ill. Be aware if the stress is affecting you and take measures to relieve it.

- If you are struggling with any aspect do not be afraid to ask for help.

- Do not spend needless hours worrying about any aspect of the job.

- If you find a working relationship difficult, try to find ways to make it better.

Also, seek out information and support if it is not forthcoming and build fun into each and every day.

Beyond any shadow of a doubt one of the reasons that Elaine survived her ordeal is her strength of character. She was determined to find a better way and to overcome her traumatic illness and stressful school circumstances. If you have the opportunity to hear Elaine speak, then I strongly advise you to go along and hear her harrowing story. She is another of those people you call survivors with spirit.

"Character isn't something you were born with and can't change, like your fingerprints. It's something you weren't born with and must take responsibility for forming." *Jim Rohn (business philosopher)*

In my personal quest to help as many people as I can to fulfil their potential, I am fortunate enough to work with all kinds of people from different backgrounds, operating in different industries and markets with different cultures and creeds.

A question I have often pondered on is: "Why are some people successful and some not?" Can it be distilled down to one difference? From my observations it is important to possess a number of qualities – passion, desire, vision and commitment are vital ingredients. However, in my opinion there is one ingredient that stands head and shoulders above the rest.

The difference is character. "Never judge a person by the amount of times they get knocked down, only by the amount of times they get back up again," is a quote I read somewhere. The vital key ingredient is persistence. You only really fail when you actually give up. Up until then you are merely going through a learning curve that influences how you react.

Successful people suffer setbacks. We all do. But the successful ones learn and apply their new learning... and then they go again. No matter who you are you cannot affect the past, you can only shape the future. Don't beat yourself up about the mistakes you have made. We have all been there and done that. Learn from your mistakes, dust yourself down, stand tall, restate your objectives and go forward confident in your abilities to overcome the obstacles that life puts in your way.

A matter of confidence

Opportunities to learn are everywhere. One evening I was watching a DVD called *The Devil Wears Prada*. It is a classic comedy drama with a happy, romantic ending. Meryl Streep plays a powerful and demanding editor of a top flight fashion magazine, who has an unrealistic work ethic both for herself and her staff.

And it made me think of a chance comment I overheard at a speaking engagement. It was a reference made about a head teacher who was so demanding that his staff could not identify with him. They seldom stayed at school for longer than was absolutely necessary, as they felt he would not appreciate their time. They certainly did not seem to hold him in high regard or with fond memories. He was an unmarried man and oblivious to the home life of his colleagues, who had family demands and commitments. He frequently said, when remonstrating with his staff: "For goodness sake, your work comes first."

How do feel about that statement? Should your work come first? Does it? How often? Have you ever encountered this sentiment? Do you think it is a valid stance to take?

Maybe the male readers will find *Prada* inappropriate for their viewing preferences. A rousing 'unisex' film is *Field of Dreams* (1989) with Kevin Costner. A professional speaker colleague, Geoff Ramm, enthuses over the power of this movie. It is a really inspirational family film – well worth a watch. More information on Geoff can be found at **www.mercurymarketing.co.uk**.

Personal compass

From time to time, our lives can and do go off balance. Occasionally, we may have to alter our compass. It is in such situations, I believe, that it is important to establish vertical alignment or VA. My personal alignment is first of all my spiritual self, secondly my family and finally my work.

The Oxford Dictionary's definition of spiritual is "of the soul or spirit". Wikipedia's explanation adds: "The path, work, practice, or tradition of perceiving and internalising one's true nature and relationship to the rest of existence."

My personal alignment of spiritual, family and work is my default position. And with this as my moral and life compass, I can confidently go off road when a serious situation arises; secure in the knowledge that my VA will kick back in once I have dealt with those things that happen to us all that can take over our lives for a period of time (I call them life attacks); things such as illness, marriage, death, birth, career and work pressures. If you have a solid foundation in your VA then you will cope much better when life attacks besiege you. You will have a safety net and it will return you to a solid and familiar routine that will comfort, satisfy and support all your needs.

So, ask yourself the following questions:

1. **Have you taken time to consider your own vertical alignment?**
2. **What is important in your life?**
3. **Have you got this set as your personal default?**

Meryl Streep was a confident leading light in *The Devil Wears Prada*, and in your life you can be too. You can change your life when you change your state of mind. Do you want to be more confident? Do you compare yourself to others unfavourably? Do you compare your weaknesses with their strengths? Many people do and little wonder that they feel less than confident.

Confident people are very relaxed. Let's consider meeting new people for example and trying to set yourself at ease in new situations. I suggest you use the acronym FORE as part of your questioning routine, ie Family, Occupation, Recreation and Education.

Use open questions to find out more information and closed questions to clarify understanding. Start conversations with open questions on the FORE topics such as: What year group do you teach? How did you find the traffic today? Which workshops are you attending? In what way can I help you? Have you had an Ofsted recently? Tell me more. Where do you plan to spend the holidays? Who? Why? For what reason? And so on. Let's face it, we all like to talk about ourselves. You will be known as a great listener and conversationalist if you use such an approach and this is a confidence booster in itself.

Nowadays, networking is an essential skill in both public and private sectors. If you attend a networking course such as those run by Will Kintish (**www.kintish.co.uk**), you will learn invaluable tips to make you more confident in dealing with people and many of these people skills focus on FORE.

You could also consider an excellent networking book by Jan Vermeiren called *Let's Connect.* (**www.janvermeiren.com**).

When you are not feeling confident you can experience symptoms of stress eg headaches, nausea and indigestion. You may breathe more quickly, perspire more, have palpitations or suffer from chest pains, tiredness, craving for food, nail biting, nervous twitches or muscle spasms. You may experience many different feelings, including anxiety, fear, anger, frustration and depression. Extreme anxiety can cause giddiness, heart palpitations, headaches or stomach pains. And longer term you may be putting yourself at risk from high blood pressure, heart attacks, strokes and impotence.

What do you want to learn about yourself right now?

Rather than allowing stress to build up I suggest you read down the list below and highlight the ones which you can action today.

Can you sign up to three action points?

1. Identify the difference between pressure and stress.

2. Complete a distress audit. (**@**)

3. Learn to say no to jobs that put you under pressure.

4. Make a list of tasks you have to do each day and set priorities.

5. Create a stop list alongside your to do list.

6. Do not leave a task until the last minute. Do it now.

7. Do not put it down. Put it away.

8. Review any addictive behaviours especially alcohol and cigarettes.

9. If you are finding yourself reaching again for the biscuit barrel or glass of wine, take a long deep breath. Physically stop yourself.

10. Set yourself realistic targets and goals – do not try to be super human – and at the same time have a huge long term goal to stretch you and keep your spirits charged. Aim high and dream big.

11. Learn to distinguish what's worth worrying about and what's not.

12. Keep in touch with your favourite friends – select a few special people and keep in touch with them regularly.

13. Talk through your challenges with someone you trust and respect rather than bottling up your feelings. Consider a coaching session.

14. Look back on the challenges of the day and realise how silly it was to get upset.

15. Take time off from pressures and responsibilities to do something totally for yourself (eg a long relaxing bath, read a magazine, take a walk etc).

16. Find a new hobby or spend more time doing one you already enjoy. Create quality time for you (and your loved ones).

17. Do one thing at a time.

18. Take one bite at a time especially when you are eating – eat slowly and savour your food.

19. Keep active – exercise is a great way of letting off steam.

20. Live in the present. Forget any anxieties for the past or future.

21. Try to pamper yourself – have a beauty or body treatment such as Indian head massage or reflexology.

22. Laugh! Smile! Have fun! Elect to be a stress free zone.

23. Join a relaxation class such as yoga and reduce tension by exercise and meditation.

24. Learn to unwind through deep breathing. Relax all the muscles in your body by tensing them, and then relax.

Look at your three highlighted points. Can you sign up to one action that you can put into place in the next 24 hours?

If so, make a note of it now and commit to it by sharing your plan with a close friend or family member. Ask them to make sure you do it.

@ This check list is available as a PDF on my website.

You could use it at a staff meeting to generate discussion or post it on the staff notice board to give reminders and encouragement.

Research has shown that optimism leads to a positive chain of events.

It also shows that Positive People:

- Live longer

- Experience fewer negative life events

- Tend to be more relaxed and therefore less likely to view events as crises

- Worry less

- Are less likely to become ill

- Are more successful.

(Seligman, 2002)

Chapter 4

Tips and goal-setting
for a more positive outlook

Stories affect our thoughts, beliefs, values, attitudes and behaviours. If you are not modelling appropriate communication with positive stories that teach, inspire, motivate, support and encourage, you can't expect those you teach and serve to do differently.

What kind of stories are heard within the walls of your school/college/university? Are they the tales of legendary leadership, outstanding staff and tales of success? Are the staff and students telling stories that uplift and reinforce the school ethos, or is it the negative gossip of a blame culture?

Optimism makes you persistent. Pessimism drains your energy and focus. Research has shown that optimism leads to a positive chain of events. It also shows that positive people:

- Live longer
- Experience fewer negative life events
- Tend to be more relaxed and therefore less likely to view events as crises
- Worry less
- Are less likely to become ill
- Are more successful.

So who would not want to be more optimistic? Research suggests that whether we are born optimists or pessimists is due largely to our parents and how we react with people is determined as follows:

60% inherited from our parents

20% learned behaviour

20% changeable. (Kivimaki et al, 2005)

Behaviour experts know that on average it takes three weeks to change behaviour and a further nine weeks to turn that new behaviour into a habit. That is why my Cool Fat Cats Strategies (which evolved from the Cool Beans Programme) talk about a 90-day programme (see Chapter 7, page 96).

Labelling Exercise: What you say when you talk to yourself

Write down five words or short phrases that could be used to describe you. Also ask a colleague and partner or friend to do the same. Once you have the five things about yourself from the three different perspectives mark each observation as a positive ☺ or as a negative ☹.

For each positive comment think of new positive words or phrases to support it. Make it your goal to put in place only positive behaviours. Share this information with your closest friends and allies. Now you have created your own personality window, when you look through it you can reinforce what you want to see.

I would recommend you read *What to say when you talk to yourself*, by Shad Helmstetter. (**@ Download my booklist as a PDF**).

Story time

Gerry Barton operates the ferry on Southampton water. Several years ago he had a daily traveller on the ferry called Tina, who worked in Superdrug. She often talked to Gerry about her son, Craig. Tina and her partner had separated when Craig was eight and he was raised by his mother. Tina believed in her son and was very proud of him. He had big dreams to make it in the music business. Gerry spoke to Tina most days and over a period of months and years as she travelled backwards and forwards on the ferry. When they chatted Tina was always cheerful and very positive about Craig's future. Gerry was unaware that Tina's son was a young singer and composer; he was crazy about writing music and she supported his ambitions. She may well have been a struggling single parent but that was not going to stop her giving Craig her full support.

One day Tina asked: "Gerry do you ever watch Top of the Pops?*" When Gerry asked: "Why?", Tina replied: "Well my son is on TV tonight, please watch it for me!"*

His name is Craig... Craig David. Funnily enough Tina doesn't travel to work at Superdrug any more.

The Law of Attraction

The Craig David story supports the Law of Attraction, which states that whatever you focus your attention on and think about most often, you attract into your life. You create circumstances and events in your life according to your dominant thoughts. Any line of thinking which you believe and on which you constantly dwell, takes root in your subconscious mind and cannot fail to influence you. Many people try to achieve their goals with their own on-board computer pre-programmed to hold them back. You have to learn to erase and replace negative attitudes. The fact is the longer a person has "bought the thought" the truer it is in their mind.

You need to learn to erase and replace negative attitudes and to see failure merely as an event and a natural step in the process of achieving your objective. You need to learn that if you fail it helps you move forward. The key difference between a multi-millionaire and a mere wealthy man is the former has been prepared to fail more often.

Are you where you want to be? Where you dreamed you'd be five years ago? The job you want? The body you want? The relationships you want? In other words, do you have the life you want?

If your answer is no, it is most likely that your excuses are keeping you from getting the results you want. Excuses that as a coach I have heard many times:

- I don't have the time
- I don't have the money
- It's too hard
- I'm too busy
- I can't help it
- Nothing ever works for me.

If these are the kinds of thoughts that run through your head when you're confronted with the things you want but don't have, then you've got the same problem as millions of others. You let your excuses talk you out of your dreams and your goals. Instead, think on the words of Henry Ford (automobile innovator and businessman): "One of the greatest discoveries a man makes, one of his great surprises, is to find he can do what he was afraid he couldn't do."

Enthusiasm is much more important than intelligence when it comes to thinking upbeat. Thinking this way creates positive energy so from now on you must be very careful what you spend time thinking about. Sometimes things do go wrong and you may question your abilities. It is then that the tide goes out and the character comes in.

"This year, I'm going to follow through on my promises to myself." Have you ever made a statement like that? Many people do, especially around the time of New Year resolutions.

You know what you need to do, what you're supposed to do and what you want to do in order to achieve your goals. Self discipline is the key to realising them and is incredibly easy to achieve. Follow the simple, tried and tested steps below:

Long-term goal

- Take time to plan. An excellent maxim is: "Well begun is half done... "

- Make notes and begin to formalise ideas

- Focus on the big picture – fine detail is not important at this stage

- Establish your goal

- Expand on why your goal is important to you

- Select a reward that you find motivating and that will be of benefit.

Personalise your screen saver with pictures of your goals. Ensure you are in the pictures. Share your goals with a power circle of close friends and family who will actively support your objectives and beware of dream stealers and negative influences. Minimise your exposure to them. Avoid pity parties; rather search out the company of like-minded friends.

Seek regular professional coaching or mentoring support. Then, with help, establish a realistic date and commit this goal to paper. Post the dated goal in prominent positions and commit to reading your goal on a daily basis. Also read aloud your goal whenever possible – this is powerful! Consider making it the welcome message on your phone.

Medium-term goal

If you want or need to change, then you need to go to places you have never been. Adopt this open-minded attitude and decide what has to be done to progress. To get promotion for example we need to be recognised. To be recognised, we need to ensure we have the skills in place to apply for the position. Therefore a mid-term goal could be to arrange to speak to the person or department at work who could help you to gain access to in-house or external training.

Next you define the medium-term goal and commit that to paper with a date. Then establish a mid-term reward – perhaps a dinner out or weekend away or a new gadget for the car or gym membership.

Short-term goal

This is where your action starts. It is said that to eat an elephant we do so one bite at a time. Take the same approach with your goals.

So, to get that promotion, volunteer and create high visibility within your organisation. Consider organising a team event for the company to increase their awareness of you. Discuss with the team the options and book the event. You could go for the triple win now; as this team event could also double up as your reward for the short-term goal. The added bonus is the recognition that will follow. Now savour the moment!

So, good luck and remember it is you that will create the change in your life.

In 2002, I was training on goal setting with staff in a school in Warrington. The head teacher, Lesley, identified a big personal goal. She wanted to be in a position to take her husband on a fabulous cruise in the Caribbean for his 40th birthday. This goal was very do-able as she had time in hand, with this landmark being some six years hence. Lesley joined my VC group. VC in this case stands for Virtual Conscience and it involves me prompting my clients with reminders and encouragement to help them stay on track. As a result of her request for help, I emailed her several times each year to check on her progress, to keep her dream alive and focus on goal targets. Imagine my delight when

Lesley contacted me recently to book me for further work and to inform me that the cruise has been arranged for next January. She has even applied for unpaid leave so that the special event coincides with the actual birthday.

Goal Setting Study

Perhaps the most revealing exposition on the importance of goals comes from a Harvard study, cited by Mark McCormack in his book *What they don't teach you in Harvard Business School.* Here is a synopsis of the study, which was conducted over ten years between 1979 and 1989.

In 1979 the graduates of the MBA programme at Harvard were asked a simple question:

"Have you set clear, written goals for your future and made plans to accomplish them?"

The results were very interesting:

- 84% had no specific goals at all
- 13% had goals but not committed to paper
- 3% had clear goals and plans that were written down.

In 1989, ten years after the first phase of the study, the graduates of that class were interviewed. Their results were even more startling:

- The 13% that had goals but not written down were earning twice as much as the 84% that did not have any goals.

An even more interesting statistic is that the 3% who had written down plans and goals were earning on average ten times more than the other 97%. The fact is that the mere act of writing a goal down on paper increased its chances of being accomplished by a staggering 90%.

"miaow, miaow, **miaow**... miaow, miaow"

Coach yourself with a
positive self-talk every day!

The problem with being perfect

Fear always lurks behind perfectionism. Confronting your fears, allowing yourself the right to be human can, paradoxically, make you a far happier and more productive person. Complete the exercise below and mark yourself according to the instructions, ie on a scale of one to ten, the higher the score the greater your degree of perfectionism.

Perfectionism Self-Assessment

I *do not accept work* that fails to meet my high personal standards

I *re-work* reports and letters until they are excellent

I *miss deadlines* because I need to fix work that is not up to scratch

I *criticise* friends and family for their poor performance

I *re-work* jobs that have been completed by others

I feel intense *embarrassment if any errors* are found in my work

I can cause *resentment* in the team because I criticise team members

I *can't bear to accept advice* or help from others

I *resist delegation* because I know I'll need to re-do the work

I *put off projects* and tasks if I have any doubt that I can do a *perfect* job

If I want a job *done properly,* I have to *do it myself*

Aim for success,
not perfection.

2	3	4	5	6	7	8	9	10

What are you putting off until tomorrow?

Focus on the italic word and score.

Again, the lower the number the better you rate yourself.

Procrastination Self-Assessment
I find it hard to *focus* and concentrate on a task
I avoid *conflict* or unpleasant situations by doing something else
I complete *easier,* low priority jobs before the tough tasks
I *miss deadlines* because less important tasks have gotten in the way
I leave *difficult tasks* to the last minute and complete them under pressure
I *don't clear and re-organise* my working area before starting a major task
I spend time *chatting* in the workplace if I feel under pressure

Your score: Perfectionism

80-110: It is unhealthy to believe that work or output that is anything less than perfect is unacceptable. Review your scoring then discuss your results with someone whose opinion you respect.

50-79: Learn to derive a real sense of pleasure from your work. Do you feel that things are never quite good enough? Aim for success, not perfection.

20-49: You are painstaking yet not compulsive with impossible goals. Are you happy with your score? You are certainly on the right track. Low 20s are good results.

Less than 20: You are not too perfect and this is good. However, beware of complacency and possible issues. Always strive for high yet realistic standards. Well done!

Procrastination prevents growth and is the best ever labour saving device. Own your decisions! So whatever needs to be done in your life, just get on with it and do it now.

Review in six week intervals.

2	3	4	5	6	7	8	9	10

Your score: Procrastination

50-70 Putting things off can result in a sense of guilt, stress and loss of personal productivity. High scores could imply that you are impeding your ability to function well. Have a realistic appreciation of your obligations, abilities and potential.

30-49 If tasks seem too big or difficult then embrace the strategies suggested in the book. You are making progress. Do one thing at a time really well and reward yourself.

10-29 You are aware of deadlines and also of how you spend your time. Generally, you feel in control of your time and have a balance within your life/ work. These are good scores. Keep focused on what you can achieve.

Less than 10 You value your time and allocate it well. Always remember to savour the moment - not everything needs to be done right now.

The Station *by Robert J Hastings*

Tucked away in our subconscious is an idyllic vision.

We see ourselves on a long trip that spans the continent.

We are travelling by trains. Out of the windows we drink in the passing scene of cars on nearby highways, of children waving, of cattle grazing, of flatlands and valleys, of mountains and rolling hillsides, of city skylines and village halls.

But uppermost in our mind is the final destination.

On a certain day at a certain hour, we will pull into the station. Bands will be playing and flags waving. Once we get there so many wonderful dreams will come true.

And the pieces of our lives will fit together like a completed jigsaw puzzle.

We pace the aisles of the train cursing the minutes spent waiting, waiting, waiting for the station!

"When we reach the station that will be it!" we cry.

"When I am 18!"

"When I buy the new 450SL Mercedes Benz!"

"When I put the last kid through university!"

"When I have paid off the mortgage!"

"When I reach the age of retirement, I shall live happily ever after!"

Sooner or later, we must realise that there is no station, no one place to arrive at once and for all. The true joy of life is the trip itself. The station is only a dream. It constantly outdistances us.

"Seize the day! Relish the moment!" is a good motto. Forget the regrets over yesterday and the fear of tomorrow. Regret and fear are twin thieves who rob us of today.

So, stop pacing the aisles and counting the miles...

Climb more mountains, eat more ice cream, go barefoot in the park, enjoy the rain on your skin and the wind in your hair, watch more sunsets, laugh more, cry less.

Life must be lived as we go along.

Top 10
Success Tips

1. Think like you want to be. It is hard to be happy, joyful and successful if you don't think that you are a happy, joyful and successful person. Think it first. Then do it! Talk it into existence. Successful sports professionals visualise themselves crossing the finishing lines and collecting the gold medals long before such events materialise. You need to adopt the same upbeat mental attitude.

2. Smile! There's no arguing with this one – research has shown that smiling has both psychological and physiological effects. So, put a smile on your face and you'll be on your way to a change in attitude!

3. Immerse yourself. Read books, articles and magazines that help you understand and adopt your new attitude. Watch films or listen to music that inspires you and encourages you to change. Purchase uplifting personal development CDs for your car and turn your vehicle into a travelling university.

4. Change your actions. It is difficult to change your attitude if you keep doing the same old stuff the same old way. Do things differently to start thinking differently. Embrace change. Consider reading *Who Moved My Cheese* or *Polar Bear Pirates*, great little books on change. Do not be fooled by their simplicity.

5. Change your environment. Make your environment reflect the attitude you wish to have. Create the physical space that makes you eager to change. Start by having a clear out. Do some life laundry. Your wardrobe is a great place to start. Many of us wear only 25% of our clothes. Be ruthless and black bag it. The charity shops will be grateful and you will feel all the better for decluttering.

6. Follow the leader. Find someone who already has the

attitude you wish to have. Follow their lead, learn from their example.

7. Help others (and help yourself). One of the fastest ways to change your attitude is to take the focus off yourself and to help others in need. Take part in a sponsored event. This is a win/win as the charity benefits for the funds and you feel better and get fitter into the bargain.

8. Get a little help from your friends and family. Contact your support network and tell them what you're doing and enlist their support to help you change and give you ideas. The more you feel like you're part of a group effort, the more likely you are to be successful.

9. Work with a pro. If the change you desire to make is a big one or is extremely radical, consider getting help from a coach. Professionals can reduce the time and frustrations involved, as well as provide you with many new ideas to help you grow.

10. Be patient. Recognise that most changes occur slowly, over an extended period of time. If you don't get immediate results, don't be surprised. Keep working, it'll come. Most importantly – don't quit! Never give up on yourself!

"I do not give you permission to upset me today!" It's all a matter of choice. In difficult situations the only person you can truly influence and control is yourself. This is a key phrase in our training courses.

(Excerpt from the Cool Beans Desktop)

Dealing with difficult people

Critical conversations

Why argue? It rarely works and really does waste your time. Better is to learn tried and tested techniques for dealing with awkward people such as loved ones, colleagues, parents or students.

When we start blaming others we give them control of the situation. Practise saying: "I am not going to allow you to upset me today!" This magic phrase keeps your self control and at the same time acknowledges your frustration and anger. In some cases it may be better to think the magic phrase as opposed to speaking it out.

It can also be developed, for example: "I am not going to upset myself today." Are you stressed about projects and workload? Is your personal life experiencing challenges? Are you tired of being tired? All of these circumstances can lead to a warped perception of reality. They can also lead to serious illness and depression so it is a good idea to deal with them effectively. Part of the purpose of difficult conversations is to raise issues about competence and performance – be these external or internal conversations. You can use such situations to reflect and renew people's commitment to the organisation.

If you overreact you may well be left with considerable damage to repair. It happens. However if you find yourself losing your temper and becoming aggressive on a regular basis it is time to take stock. Pay attention to what is really going on in your life. Manage your emotions. Listen to your mind. It will tell you what is warranted and you can avoid most potentially difficult and dangerous situations this way.

> **If you wish to, download an information sheet called Desirable Traits (@). It highlights the benefits of skills such as listening, empathising, asking the right questions plus the power of a winning smile (when appropriate).**

Active listening

"Courage is what it takes to stand up and speak; courage is also what it takes to sit down and listen." *Winston Churchill*

Listening is a very under-rated skill. When we understand how simple interactions work, we can use them to build rapport. We have to understand the other person. Neuro-Linguistic Programming (NLP) is one method that can assist you to do this.

I studied NLP during my coaching diploma and I learned as much if not more as a child watching my mother interact with others. As a good teacher I strongly suspect that you may unconsciously employ NLP in the classroom. My coaching certification certainly supported and consolidated my personal experiences.

For example, I have developed a relationship of mutual respect and trust with one of my clients to a point where, during a session, she told me about her imminent IVF treatment. She voiced concerns. She was very nervous and feared the unknown. Without thinking, I matched her tone. She leant forward to give me very personal information and I matched her body language and unconsciously mirrored her facial expressions. The client and I used similar pitch and pace within our speech patterns. For me, this is an automatic response, as I am able to call on my people skills. If you are not confident in this way, then I suggest you consider attending basic NLP training. By so doing you may develop a better understanding of what goes on between yourself and others – figuring out how they think, realising what they want and understanding what makes them tick. I gave my client time to voice her concerns using active listening skills and empathy. I then suggested a way forward and, as a result, my client left happier and more relaxed about her future.

Little things – like active listening – do make a big difference. They are the first rule of diffusing difficult situations. If you have an angry parent arrive at school, chances are they simply want to talk to someone they respect, someone who will listen to them.

Chapter 5

Contributions, observations and opinions
from education professionals

There is a quote, attributed to Sir Isaac Newton (physicist, mathematician, astronomer and philosopher). It alludes to "standing on the shoulders of giants". With the contributions and support I have received in producing this book I feel that I, too, have had such an opportunity. I have been pleased to acknowledge these sources throughout the book. I hope the following contributions prove useful:

Interview with Jacqui

Jacqui is 39 years of age and married with three children. She has been teaching for 18 years for Glasgow City Council, has taught at every stage of primary school and is currently on the fast track programme to headship. She has also taught nursery classes during her time as a supply teacher.

Q. What is the most difficult situation you have had to deal with in your teaching career? Outline the circumstances:

There were many challenges but probably the most stressful was while my husband was setting up his own business as a restaurateur. We had financial pressures and childcare problems.

Prior to my husband's venture I had been job sharing for four years while my children were pre-school age. I loved the work/life balance that this provided and I had the perfect job-share partner. With my husband not working it meant I had to go back to work full-time. My youngest daughter was only 16 months and her Dad became house husband, child minder, entrepreneur and managing director.

I couldn't get a permanent contract, so I was working two or three days job-share permanent at my original post and doing supply work covering any school or class that needed me.

Let me tell you, the first year was not easy! I was in some of the roughest areas in Glasgow, high areas of deprivation, with children whose teachers had been off work with long-term stress. The schools had lists of supply teachers in and out of classes. So there was no continuity and very little discipline.

I had chairs thrown at me, I was sworn at regularly, with our council's inclusion policy I often had children with special needs, ie autistic, blind, dyspraxic, ADHD. Often there was no support teacher or suitable information about a child's specific learning needs. You truly saw a lot of poor/bad practice. Fortunately you also saw some good.

After struggling through this difficult time, I eventually found another school. They were so desperate to have a reliable long-term temporary teacher to provide cover for their senior teachers that they reframed their vacancy in the GCC Bulletin, so that I could apply. I ended up with two job-share posts.

The head teacher had to fight tooth and nail to keep me in post. It was not the council's policy to let one teacher hold down two job-shares. But as no one else applied and it had been sitting vacant for over two years with a stream of different supply teachers, the council eventually gave in to common sense and lobbying from staff and parents.

I continued to work between two schools for two years. I had to plan for the entire primary curriculum, as I was teaching all stages on different days of the week.

I remember spending hours every evening organising lessons. This was so tiring and my own family was being ignored. It was time to prioritise.

Q. How did you deal with these very hard times?

I took time to reflect on my situation and decided to prioritise what was important to me. My husband helped me.

Q. What assistance/support did you get from the education authority/your head teacher?

None from authority. If anything they made things very difficult. I was constantly on the phone to them, nearly every day, usually seeking work but also sorting out mistakes in pay etc – adding stress to an already stressful job. Head teachers in most schools were very helpful.

Q. What worked and what didn't?

Job-sharing between the two schools worked in my second year, once I knew I was on a long-term contract and I could plan more effectively with colleagues and the head teacher in both schools.

Q. What have you learned from these experiences?

That you need to plan family time into your work schedule, for your own sanity. You are only a small cog in the wheel as far as the authority is concerned. Make quality time for yourself as this helps you to de-stress and refocus on your work. I learned the vital skill of time management.

Q. How can others benefit from your experience?

Take time to reflect and review your work/life balance because it is very easy for the balance to shift in favour of work as your career progresses.
Make sure that you have quality me time every week!

Q. Can you list your key success strategies for dealing with future issues (things to share with others in similar circumstances)?

1. Always have a positive outlook, things usually aren't as bad as they seem, so celebrate your triumphs, and don't just reflect on the negative.

2. Smile, it costs you nothing and you will brighten up the day.

3. Keep a well ordered diary, but don't just use it for work related matters, check that you have your "me" time in there too![1]

Visit **www.eilidhmilnes.com** and select 'Organised Mum' for a wide range of planners, pocket diaries, school and family organisers.

[1] **The latest news on Jacqui is that she is doing extremely well. She is planning a Comenius project. (See Chapter 2, page 26 for web link and information.)**

The thoughts of Ann Griffiths, head teacher

On being yourself

When you are a young teacher you are the recipient of quite a lot of confusing advice: "Never smile until Christmas, or even until Easter", according to my hard-bitten, cynical secondary teacher husband. "Remember you are there to teach, not to be liked."

However, it took me a long time to realise that in order to be a better teacher you have to show a human side so that the children can relate to you as a person. Showing a sense of humour definitely helps with relationships. Taking time to listen to innumerable anecdotes of happenings that are important to the children is crucial, albeit exhausting. The difficulty is getting the balance right; too soft and approachable can create problems for some children in thinking that they do not have to conform to rules and can ignore you, particularly as children become older. You do need to adopt different strategies depending on the age of the children. When I switched to years one and two, it took a while to realise that they did not understand irony and took everything literally. Older juniors can work with more freedom, wider parameters and humour.

On techniques

Most teachers develop the look, the tone, the ability to see behind or around them with peripheral vision and extra sensitive hearing. Confidence is key; I have seen young teachers get better but some are just not suited mentally to that belief that they are in charge; weak voices, faltering looks including blind terror like rabbits in headlights spring to mind. I think body language training should be mandatory for all new and supply teachers.

On the job

On a good day when a child makes that leap, tells you that you are the best teacher they have ever had, or in my case the "best boss person", and parents come up to thank you, then it is the best job in the world. Every teacher will tell you that it is worthwhile to make a difference to how a child feels about themselves, developing confidence to try something and achieve something new.

On a bad day, the pressure is unrelenting and exhaustion and frustration kick in. The children sense it and it becomes worse

– windy days make it worse too. Wind can make people bad tempered. If we feel bad at the start of the day and carry in personal baggage we don't have the emotional energy to give to the children and then it is more difficult. Often this leads to illness. Supportive colleagues and, hopefully, a supportive head are crucial here to be alert to this. They should take care to support struggling teachers, including encouraging them to take a break or even telling them to go home.

I recently had a young teacher who told me that despite the distance she still travels to work at my school because she felt supported by colleagues and me – that felt very humbling. I also feel that only teachers truly understand the feeling that they never have any down time – they always work evenings, weekends, holidays and feel guilty if they don't! Head teachers seem to be even worse.

We all need outlets to relieve stress. I urge staff to go home early, take up outside interests, provide inset days to write reports, minimise the amount of paperwork, even bring in cakes. Unfortunately I worked in schools where unrealistic demands are placed on staff, where paperwork and data are gods, everyone is too busy, and new staff are isolated with "don't sit in that chair". No wonder they give up or become ill. It is difficult to know how to shift negative cultures. I am a great believer that positive people help create positive working environments. The climate is key and needs to be monitored with people who can alert leaders to changes in the wellbeing barometer.

I love many things about schools that can't be bottled. The sound of singing when children are enjoying themselves, the sound of laughter in the playground, the buzz of a productive working classroom, smiles, the pleasure of a quick unsolicited hug from a young child when he sees you, the look of pride on a child's face when they have performed in the play or spoken when they didn't think they could.

I know your book will inspire many but coping day in and day out with a smile on your face even if you feel rotten is just not for everyone and this should be acknowledged.

Philip Whiston is a primary teacher with some great ideas to share

Well done greeting

The idea of a greeting for when the children come in was an idea that was introduced to me via a superb teaching assistant I work with. We use smartboards in every classroom and frequently these will have a timetable displayed on them. This helps with organisation and adds some structure to the children's day. A greeting proved to be a more motivational tool. The text would be a celebration of a certain child. Some simple clipart, such as clapping hands or balloons, was added to the page. The text was made colourful, perhaps with some stars around it.

It may have been that a certain piece of work stood out. If this was the case a message would be displayed such as: "Well done David for producing a superb piece of work in numeracy. He really understands division now!" Obviously, this worked well for children in need of a confidence boost.

Alternatively, we had the option of displaying group messages such as, "Star group made us all proud by improving their mental arithmetic scores!"

Football team successes, netball games and certificates all made their way onto our board. I took care to celebrate improvement as a mark of achievement, rather than high-scores.

The benefits of this idea are obvious. For many of the class self-esteem can be built in certain areas. We show that we value effort, dedication and improvement. It allows us to make every child feel special.

An added benefit was that the smartboard faced the windows. Parents dropping off children in the morning could also see if their child had been mentioned. They were made aware of how we valued positive contributions and attitude.

Achievement boards

I use a smartboard almost exclusively now, as I find them far more versatile for my teaching. I do have a large whiteboard along one wall though. We turned this into a powerful tool for positive reinforcement of our school values. I printed out A5 sized certificates with smiley faces, rosettes, trophies and the like on them. Every time the children did something of note that we felt needed celebrating, we filled out one of these certificates and attached it to the board. We ensured that reasons such as being a good friend, helping someone out when they were struggling in class, sharing, achievement in sport or music, etc were noted, rather than straightforward academic success. This ensured that the children who sometimes do not get full marks could feel equally as valued in class. As mentioned above, improvement was celebrated over high marks.

We developed this idea further soon after starting it. One of the children asked if they could recommend a friend. This struck me as a superb idea, as peer praise has always appeared more powerful a reward. This had the added benefit of creating a good feeling in the class as it fostered class relations. Not all recommendations came from expected sources. Sometimes children got noticed by children they did not previously consider close friends.

Any child or adult who visited would be able to view them. Parents during parents' evening were made aware of how we valued success in class. It was always nice if they spotted their own child's name in lights!

Traffic lights

Our school is very interested in self-assessment. We feel that children setting their own targets is very important in order that they can achieve them. A useful tool I use is the traffic lights system. At the end of a piece of work, children are asked to colour in or draw a small square. This indicates their level of comfort and ease with the task. A green square indicates that they understand the task and want to move on to something new. An amber square indicates that more practice is required, possibly with support. A red square means the child has struggled and needs some help.

After coaching the children understand that a red square does not indicate failure. In fact, it shows strength and honesty to admit that they need help.

I use a standard register book to track progress throughout the week. It is nice to see lots of squares change from red to amber and then green throughout the week! It also allows me to reflect on future teaching. If a child struggled through a topic, with support, I know not to waste any time when we revisit. It prepares me to differentiate and add adult support to those who require it more efficiently.

Obviously the benefits of child centred assessment are manifold. As a teacher, it highlights progress or lack of it. For the children, it means they can access help reliably and quickly. Parents know that their child is properly cared for. It has revolutionised my marking and planning.

Thumbs up

Developed from the above concept, mid lesson children are asked to put their hands up to indicate comprehension and comfort with what I am teaching. Thumbs up indicates that they understand totally. Thumbs down indicates that they need more examples or more support. If they are unsure or simply not confident enough to start work they can wiggle their fingers in a so-so fashion. Very quickly I can assess my teaching and alter it accordingly.

Children need lots of coaching in the concept of honesty and avoiding peer-pressure. Much of this stems from the teacher. If they know that we value progress, then admitting they are not sure allows me to help. Importantly, I monitor my tone of voice and body language to ensure thumbs down are not met with silent signals of disapproval from me.

This adds to the inclusive atmosphere of the class and helps the feeling of being like one big family – a team that is working towards the same goals. Hopefully, the children I teach feel that it is OK to be wrong, to make mistakes, and to ask for help.

Special table

One concept that proved to be very popular was that of the special table. Teachers throughout the school were allowed to select a member of the class whom they felt deserved some recognition. This could be for outstanding work, excellent attitude, or perhaps an improvement to their effort in class. These children were allowed to sit on a special table in the dining hall during lunch break. A teacher sat with them to add some significance to the occasion. This sent a signal to the children that the staff cared about celebrating achievement and were willing to commit to the system of recognition. That staff member received a free meal from the caterers as a way of saying thank you. In addition, the table had a tablecloth, superior cutlery and plastic wine glasses – filled with red cordial of course. The lunchtime staff would come and take the diners' orders and wait on them.

Although some of this sounds rather silly, the children really enjoyed it and the difference to their self-esteem was easy to see. It was a clear and prominent signal to the school that we celebrated those that deserved recognition.

You could even consider having happiness classes at school. Wellington School, an impressive public school, teaches its students to identify their feelings and have developed wellbeing classes that students call happiness classes. Girls and boys in years 10 and 11 (aged 14+ and 15+) have a 40-minute timetabled lesson on the skills of wellbeing every fortnight. The lessons will give them an understanding of what factors help a life to thrive and flourish, as well as teaching them some practical skills for everyday use. I know that wellbeing and happiness are harder to measure than the 3Rs and so less attractive to state sector schools, which are built on the concept of measuring success, but I urge you to consider the example set by Wellington and share these natural highs with your students and colleagues alike.

The special table – a variation

By Mel Cooper (Year 6 class teacher)

The idea was originally introduced to help to improve relationships in the dining room between the children and the dinner ladies, who are now known as MDAs (midday assistants).

The MDAs would spend the week looking out for children who were behaving particularly well – helping younger children, being polite to each other and the staff, etc.

Thursday lunchtimes the MDAs would bring the dining room to total silence and announce the names of the children that had impressed them most over the week. Each week there would be one child from each year group selected. A list was kept to make sure that the children who were always good weren't overlooked.

The rest of the children were always genuinely pleased for the selected seven children and the whole dining room would erupt with applause after the names had been announced. They would also take time to congratulate them individually. These children were congratulated once again in the Friday morning assemblies, when they would be presented with a certificate.

The MDAs would set a table for these children for Friday lunchtime. There was a tablecloth and napkins to match, place mats, a bunch of silk flowers in a vase and even plastic wine glasses. The children would have place names made that they would keep as a souvenir. As these children arrived into the hall they would be shown to their place and, if they were having a packed lunch, would have their lunch set out for them on proper plates and their drinks poured into the glasses. The children that were having a school dinner would go to the front of the queue and have their dinner served, once again, onto proper plates.

This group of children were waited on by the MDAs and there would always be a special guest that would join them. This would be a member of staff who would agree to sit and eat their lunch with the children.

This idea worked really well from many perspectives:

- The MDAs enjoyed doing something positive for the children

- The children loved the idea of being special and eating like they were in a restaurant

- The behaviour in the dining room improved

- The children were always positive about the selected few – there was never any resentment.

Even the teaching staff enjoyed being included as a special guest.

Notes: _____

_____

_____

_____

_____

_____

"Children should live with champions and heroes"

(Excerpt from the Cool Beans Desktop)

David Hyner is a friend and colleague in the Professional Speakers' Association

He is also the parent of an autistic child

"One day at around 4am (a usual time to get up when you have a small child with autism as they rarely have normal sleep patterns), my young boy of some two and a half years was watching television," says David.

"He was standing almost nose to the screen of the television and was stimming frantically. This is an expression used to describe the energetic waving of arms and excited 'ah ah ah!' sounds that autists do when excited, as many can't talk or indeed communicate much in the traditional ways expected of a young boy.

"I'm not sure what made me do what happened next other than wanting, longing to have more connection with my son. I got down on my knees next to him and put my face next to his and stimmed like 'a good un' next to him. I confess that it was not an altogether unpleasant experience. I laughed and smiled at my son. What happened next will stay with me forever.

"My son stopped what he was doing, turned to face me and after a momentary pause proceeded to laugh with all his might at me. He then held my hand and carried on as if nothing had happened. In that moment not only did I cry like a child with the emotions of true connection, but learnt there and then that it is vital to connect to what you say and do when working with young people.

"Since that day whenever I speak or train, there is no showing off and certainly no nervousness as I connect to my delivery. The results are born out in the action taken by high school students and teachers as a result of my work.

"One example is when I trained a group of 'notorious' young men at a local high school and at the end of my talk the alpha male (a student that all the teachers had warned me about due to his behaviour and levels of disruption) shouted out to me: 'So what's the most amazing thing you've ever done then?'

"His words were meant as a challenge as I had been telling them how they could achieve big goals if they put their minds to taking action on achieving amazing things. My head wanted to say any one of the things I would have normally said at that point including running my own business, trekking in Peru and China, swimming with sharks, etc.

"My heart, however, insisted that I try the authentic connection again, so I looked him in the eye and with all my soul I said: 'My friend, the most amazing thing that I have ever done is simply to love my son with all my heart.' The silence was deafening and I heard that little voice in my head say something like: 'They're going to kill you for saying that.'

"Instead after just a second or two the tough student nodded his head and began to applaud. Within a heartbeat, the whole room echoed to the sound of applause and a few even gave me a standing ovation. At that moment I felt the power of connection. If you are nervous, you are selling yourself and your students/ delegates short, and if you are driven by ego you may (as I used to be) appear to be a show off with little conviction or authority.

"When you truly connect with your message, you are naturally more expressive, and at once your audience responds to you. Be more passionate, I dare you!"

> "Life's real heroes and heroines bear their own burdens bravely and give a helping hand to those around them."
>
> **These words are written on a plaque above the front door of Ivy cottage, a house in my village. The property was built by the Yoxall Trust in 1905.**

Thank you to all the people who took time to share their ideas and experiences. I believe each in his or her own way is a hero. I hope you agree.

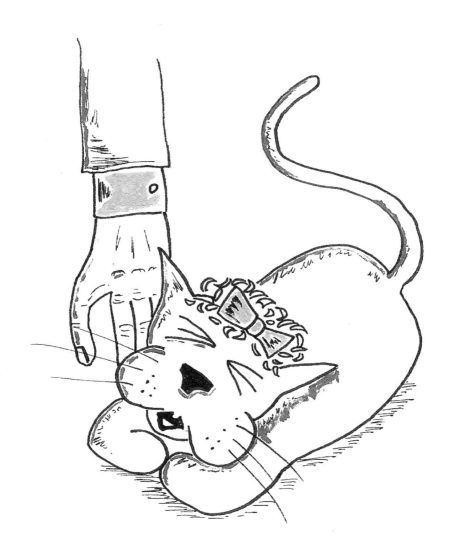

Good morning,
gorgeous!

Chapter 6

Ideas to make your day fun

- -

"An adult laughs on average 15 times a day. A young child an average of 400 times per day. Yield to the child within you."
Anonymous.

Smile

You are responsible for your attitudes and one of the most basic and important things you do for your own self-image and self-belief is smile. Go ahead, smile at the pages of this book right now!

Research is now proving that people with a good positive attitude and who smile and laugh a lot also live longer. Perhaps you feel I am stating the obvious. I would argue that from the number of glum faces I see every day in companies and car parks that is it obvious that many people are either ignorant or ignoring this basic fact.

Pay attention to how you react to things and determine how you want to respond and how you would like to react differently. How much do you care about what others think about you? Is their assessment factual or flawed? Are you emotionally attached to a fact that is not necessarily accurate?

Be a mind leader and programme your mind to think happy thoughts. If you are not leading the voices in your own head and conducting yourself in a positive fashion then you are probably not giving your best to the children in your care. You have the title of teacher and this requires leading others to be better. The degree to which you lead yourself will determine your ability to influence your students and to make a real difference in the lives of others.

Give thanks

"Gratitude is not only the greatest of virtues, but the parent of all the others." *Cicero (Roman statesman and philosopher).*

According to Emmons & McCullough, gratitude is the forgotten factor in their research on happiness (2003). In this research, under the heading *Measuring the Grateful Disposition*, most people who reported being grateful (average rating of nearly six on a seven-point scale), also had a sense of:

Wellbeing: Grateful people report higher levels of positive emotions, life satisfaction, vitality and optimism and lower levels of depression and stress. The disposition towards gratitude appears to enhance pleasant feelings more than it diminishes unpleasant emotions. Grateful people do not deny or ignore the negative aspects of life.

Prosociality: People with a strong disposition towards gratitude have the capacity to be empathic and to take the perspective of others. They are rated as more generous and more helpful by people in their social networks.

Spirituality: Those who regularly attend religious services and engage in religious activities such as prayer or reading religious material are more likely to be grateful. Grateful people are more likely to acknowledge a belief in the interconnectedness of all life and a commitment and responsibility to others.

Materialism: Grateful individuals place less importance on material goods; they are less likely to judge their own and others success in terms of possessions accumulated; they are less envious of wealthy persons; and are more likely to share their possessions with others relative to less grateful persons.

In my experience, I have found that keeping a log book helps clients to focus on positive experiences and I am pleased that this opinion is supported in the research findings: "In an experimental comparison, those who kept gratitude journals on a weekly basis exercised more regularly, reported fewer physical symptoms, felt better about their lives as a whole, and were more optimistic about the upcoming week compared to those who recorded hassles or neutral life events."

Gratitude log book: _____

_____
_____
_____
_____
_____
_____
_____
_____
_____
_____
_____
_____
_____
_____
_____
_____
_____
_____
_____
_____
_____
_____
_____
_____
_____
_____
_____
_____

Why not keep a diary for a month and note down all the good things that happen in your life? You will find that you have a lot to be grateful for.

Here are some ideas to get you started:

37 natural highs

1. Laughing till it hurts

2. A special glance or wink

3. Getting snail mail

4. Hearing your favourite song on the radio

5. Lying in bed – listening to the rain outside

6. Luxury warm towels on the towel rail

7. Finding the top you really, really want is on sale for half price

8. Chocolate of any kind

9. A long distance phone call on Skype with video

10. A bubble bath

11. Giggling

12. A good conversation

13. Any beach – anywhere

14. Finding money in a pocket or purse that you had forgotten all about

15. Skipping through autumn leaves

16. Laughing for absolutely no reason at all

17. Having someone tell you that you're beautiful – say hello gorgeous to yourself too!

18. Falling in love and your first kiss

19. Accidentally overhearing someone say something nice about you

20. Making new friends or spending time with old ones

21. Playing with a new puppy or kitten

22. Having someone play with your hair

23. Waking up from a sweet dream

24. Swinging on swings

25. Cuddling up on a couch with someone you love

26. Finding the song lyrics printed inside your new CD

27. Running downhill

28. Making eye contact with an attractive stranger

29. Winning a really competitive game

30. Preparing food with friends in the kitchen

31. Just holding hands with someone you care about

32. Meeting an old friend and realising that some things never change

33. Hugging someone you are fond of

34. Laughing at yourself

35. Watching the expression on someone's face as they open your special gift to them

36. Watching the sunrise... or the sunset

37. Jumping out of bed every morning and giving thanks for another beautiful day.

• •

Keep the attitude of a child and look for the natural highs in your life. You will become a people magnet and people will always want to spend time in your company because you make them happier.

And be grateful for what you have for, as George Simmel (German sociologist) said: "Gratitude is the moral memory of mankind." And why not commit random acts of kindness and believe in angels?

• •

Go skip!

Revisit your childhood today and do something different, something out of the ordinary and silly and fun, something childlike – just for you and just for the heck of it! Many people take life far too seriously and miss out on so many simple pleasures. Don't be one of them.

"In every real man a child is hidden that wants to play,"
Friedrich Nietzsche, German philosopher.

As for me? I am going to be skipping through today and having a lot of fun in the process. Why don't you join me?

"Life is way too serious to be taken too seriously,"
Dr Gunars Neiders, author and psychologist.

See things differently!

These thoughts are like my Cool Beans statements. They make me smile. Thank you to the client who thought to email them to me.

Select a thought for today from the list below. If things go wrong re-run the thought in your mind to keep you upbeat:

1. Accept that some days you're the pigeon, and some days you're the statue.

2. Always keep your words soft and sweet, just in case you have to eat them.

3. Always read stuff that will make you look good if you die in the middle of it.

4. Drive carefully. It's not only cars that can be recalled by their maker.

5. If you can't be kind, at least have the decency to be vague.

6. If you lend someone £20 and never see that person again, it was probably worth it.

7. It may be that your sole purpose in life is simply to serve as a warning to others.

8. Never buy a car you can't push.

9. Never put both feet in your mouth at the same time, because then you won't have a leg to stand on.

10. Nobody cares if you can't dance well. Just get up and dance.

11. Since it's the early worm that gets eaten by the bird, sleep late.

12. The second mouse gets the cheese.

13. When everything's coming your way, you're in the wrong lane.

14. Birthdays are good for you. The more you have, the longer you live.

15. You may be only one person in the world, but you may also be the world to one person.

16. Some mistakes are too much fun to only make once.

17. We could learn a lot from crayons. Some are sharp, some are pretty, some are dull, some have weird names and all have different colours, but they all live in the same box.

18. A truly happy person is one who can enjoy the scenery on a detour.

Notes: _____

_____

_____

_____

_____

_____

_____

_____

_____

_____

Share experiences

Shared experiences are powerful and can be varied. One head teacher I know gives all her staff a book to read when they join her school. This way they can all literally be working from the same page. Her book of choice is *Tuesdays with Morrie* by Mitch Albom. Another took her staff to Dublin for a team building inset day.

Whatever you choose as your shared experience, take time to savour moments with your team and find out how it impacted on them as individuals. We are all different. Some people will shine and others reflect. "There are two ways of spreading light: to be the candle or the mirror that reflects it," Edith Wharton (novelist and designer). You will find details of Mitch Albom's book and many others on the Booklist PDF (@).

Some readers already subscribe to my quarterly newsletter (@). Email is a popular communication medium for me. I receive a great many emails each day. Some fall into the trash or junk category and then occasionally someone does me a favour by forwarding a gem. The following list of tips actually came in on an email so sadly I cannot give credit to the author. Suffice to say, I think the tips are also useful ideas.

Top Tips for staying Youthful!

1. Throw out non-essential numbers. This includes age, weight, and height. Let the doctors worry about them.

2. Keep only cheerful friends. Moaning minnies and negative people only pull you down. (Please keep this in mind if you are sometimes one of those grumpies! Do your friends really want to share all your negative opinions?) Look for firelighters, ie people who will support and help you, or friends who will fan the flames of your success.

3. Keep learning. Learn more about the computer, crafts, gardening or whatever appeals to you. Never let the brain get idle. "An idle mind is the devil's workshop. And the devil's name is Alzheimer's!" (*Anonymous*).

4. Enjoy the simple things... list these for yourself now:

_____

_____

_____

_____

_____

_____

_____

_____

_____

5. Laugh often, long and loud. Laugh until you gasp for breath. If you have friends who make you laugh, spend lots and lots of time with them. Feed on their happy spirits.

6. The tears happen. Endure, grieve and then move on. Live while you are alive. The only person who is with us our entire life is ourself.

7. Surround yourself with what you love. Whether it's family, pets, keepsakes, music, plants, hobbies or whatever makes you happy. Enjoy your home, it can be your refuge and sanctuary.

8. Cherish your health. If it is good, preserve it. If it is unstable, improve it. If it is beyond what you can improve, get help.

"If you don't think it's a great day, try missing one!"
Zig Ziglar (motivational speaker and author).

9. Don't take guilt trips. Take a trip to a shopping centre, a car forecourt or even to a foreign country, but not to where the guilt is. Or view guilt differently – **G U I L T Y**

Get **U** (yourself) **I**ndulgent **L**eisure **T**ime **Y**es! **Y**ahoo! **Y**ippee!

10. Tell the people you love, that you love them – at every opportunity. Start with yourself! Good morning gorgeous!

Seven ways to be
a Cool Fat Cat...

...want to survive the system?

Good morning
gorgeous!

Be more likeable

Be a good
finder!

Improve today, to make a better tomorrow

Get better
not bitter!

Find out if bitterness is preventing a better tomorrow

Stay positive!

Check where your self-talk is taking you

You'll catch more
with sugar than vinegar!

Encourage people to want to work with you

Charge!
Take a risk!

Feel bold and brave

Use your
stop list!

Use your stop list today, to help with your to do list tomorrow

Eilidh Milnes: Email: e@eilidhmilnes.com Telephone: +44 (0) 1270 212 999 Website: www.eilidhmilnes.com

Chapter 7

Strategies for a happy, less stressed life

- -

"Life is either a daring adventure or nothing." *Helen Keller, author, activist and lecturer.*

When I published Cool Beans, the positive person's desktop, little did I realise the impact it could have. I have received countless emails, phone calls, texts and letters telling me that the Cool Beans sayings have been powerful and inspired life changes. This encouraged me so much that it was instrumental in the writing of *Love your life - survive the system.*

If you were to ask me why I decided to create Cool Beans, the most simple and honest answer would be that I wanted to honour the memory of my mother. She was the most outstanding woman I have ever known and I wanted to share her guide to life with my readers.

One thing she taught me was when you share stories and anecdotes about your family members or experiences you have had, two things happen. Firstly, your listeners connect with you on a very personal and universal level, making the message more understandable. Secondly, your stories allow them to remember and share their own stories, from which other lessons can be learned, histories revealed and relationships built. Story telling is an extraordinary gift. It is a gift that good teachers all have in common.

Our stories are our culture and the various cultures in which we participate shape our behaviours. The Bible, the Koran and other spiritual books are all based on storytelling.

What stories are being shared in your school? What is the culture of your organisation? It will be revealed in the stories you hear being retold again and again. Are you encouraging your students and colleagues with uplifting stories? If you do, your staff and students, not to mention your friends and family, will connect more appropriately, bond more successfully, change more quickly, share more openly and learn more easily. They will also remember the stories long after the facts and figures are forgotten.

The seven CFCs – The seven Cool Fat Cat strategies

All of the Cool Beans sayings (which evolved to be the Cool Fat Cats) can be seen as affirmations. As such, they are a great tool when it comes to creating change. Their power is not only in their ability to see situations and circumstances for you to achieve your goals but they also help you eliminate negative thinking.

- **Don't put it down... put it away!** Hilda was my son's first head teacher, now retired. In her words: "I am not the most tidy of people at home and your Cool Beans has been so helpful. It reminds me on a daily basis to keep things in order."

- **Take a few risks.** This is another principle that seems to have made an impact. Some years ago a delegate of mine had been so moved by this concept she went home to her husband, shared it with him and gave him a Cool Beans desktop as an encouraging gift. Within a matter of days he had resigned from his job and started his own company. Taking such big steps is a risky business, however it is also very exciting and incredibly bold. He charged!

  The last I heard his business was flourishing, he is happier, much more confident and is doing very well indeed. What a great story with a powerful message.

- **Create a stop list alongside your to do list!** So many of us are constantly making lists of things to do that have almost become an obsession. We have lists for everything from shopping, work and social life. When was the last time you had a completely clear list-free day? One way to make more time is to create a **halt list** – a list of things you are going to stop doing. Some obvious things that come to mind include:

  - **Stop** ironing – delegate or contract out
  - **Stop** watching so much television – be selective
  - **Stop** saying yes when you really mean no
  - **Stop** being late
  - **Stop** eating too fast – create time to savour and enjoy your food
  - **Stop** racing around – hurry slowly.

- **Save 10%.** Cool Beans says: "Save 10% of all your income streams…"

To quote Charles Dickens in Mr Micawber: "Annual income twenty pounds, annual expenditure nineteen and six, result happiness. Annual income twenty pounds, annual expenditure twenty pounds and six pence, result misery."

And as my Cool Beans quote goes on to say: "Money is a tool – learn to be a craftsman."

It may not always be easy but if the 'save 10%' maxim becomes your life standard the results will far outweigh any short-term discomfort.

- **Hello Gorgeous.** This is my standard greeting to my husband, my family and me. I could notice things that are less than perfect in my appearance – the development of wrinkles, the grey hair, the double chin or the expanding waistline. However, what good would that do? Instead I opt to encourage others and myself with positive statements. I elect to see fine lines and silver hair, and I smile and laugh out loud as I do a few facial exercises in the mirror. Be kind to yourself. Encourage yourself with genuine words of praise. We all have good points. Reinforce them with an inspiring phrase.

- **Be a good finder.** Look for the good in all situations. I extol you to make every effort to make this so. Affirmations have been around for centuries and I can't think of a single self-help course or book that doesn't touch on the subject in one form or another. To create affirmations focus on what you want not on what you don't want.

- **You'll always get more with sugar than you do with vinegar** is the Cool Beans version of the old adage that it is better to use a carrot rather than a stick. As teachers, I think we are all well aware of the power of words. We need to be careful not to get hung by the tongue as it is a powerful muscle.

Follow these seven Cool Fat Cat strategies and see the changes and improvements in your life.

What are you going to do today...

1. To be more likeable?

   Good morning gorgeous!

2. To improve today and make a better tomorrow?

   Be a good finder!

3. To find out if bitterness from yesterday is spoiling today and preventing a better tomorrow?

   You either get bitter or you get better!

4. To check where your self-talk is taking you?

   Coach yourself with positive self-talk every day!

5. To encourage people to want to work with you?

   You'll always get more with sugar than you do with vinegar!

6. To feel bold and brave?

   Charge! Take a risk!

7. To help you achieve your to do list tomorrow?

   Create a stop list alongside your to do list!

You need to be honest with yourself and make a pact with your conscience. You need to sign up to this as a serious commitment and post the seven Cool Fat Cats principles in visible places such as your fridge door or in your diary so that you see the simple concepts on a daily basis. If you follow these thought processes for 90 successive days I guarantee that you will see a transformation in your life.

However, if you miss a day you must return to day one and start the process all over again. I have used this technique over and over again to my advantage and I am only too well aware of how hard it is to get to day 62, miss a day and have to return to day one!

"Dream as if you'll live forever. Live as if you'll die tomorrow" *James Dean*

(Excerpt from the Cool Beans Desktop)

More information is available from the website,
where you can purchase a discounted desktop
and receive a free Cool Fat Cats action card.
(Insert code 'LYLpromoAC' when prompted at the shopping
cart. This promotional offer is available while stocks last.)

Take
risks

Chapter 8

Respect

• •

According to Wikipedia, the free online encyclopedia: "Respect is taking into consideration the views and desires of others and incorporating it into your decisions. Being truthful to people. When you respect another, you factor in and weigh others' thoughts and desires into your planning and balance it into your decision-making."

Education is our wealth but do we respect it? When I was working in the Gulf, I had the delight of spending time with a young man about the same age as my own son. He is called Ali Alsaloom. He attended a conference in Dubai in 2006, heard me speak and we have been developing a friendship ever since. He has diverse interests and his passion for life is his particular fuel.

Education is communicating and to communicate with others you first need to respect, is Ali's view on life. He told me a tale about an experience he had had in a school. Something else I appreciate about the Middle Eastern cultures is their liking for stories. I subsequently asked Ali to write up his narrative and here is his story for you now.

Ali's story

Respect is the keyword in any healthy educational system and that's why in the Middle East a teacher, or as we say Almu'alem, is highly appreciated, loved and most importantly highly respected. However, in order to sustain a strong solid circle of respect, the teacher must make no mistake that is related to respect.

I was invited by a government educational college in my city, Abu Dhabi, to deliver a presentation about my educational experience. I accepted the invitation. I did not ask about the participants' background or age.

When I entered the conference room, there were over 400 male and female students between 16 and 20 years old. Unfortunately, I felt as if I had just entered a kindergarten as most of the students were making noises, talking to each other. Some were just walking in front of me leaving the conference room and the rest were just whispering with their classmates. They were probably laughing or talking about me. Oh yeah, it was a disaster!

I was the second presenter. I noticed that more than half of the students were not giving the first speaker their full attention, nor respecting his topic. Most probably they were not able to understand his sophisticated words, which were far beyond their level of English understanding. I decided to ask the college organiser if I was allowed to say a few words in Arabic before I delivered my presentation in English and that was very much accepted.

While I was introduced to the students in the room, I could still hear loud noises coming from each corner of the room until the very moment when I took the microphone and spoke the following phrase in Arabic: "Besmellah alrahman alraheem," which means "In the name of Allah, All Merciful, the Mercy-Giving". It is a blessing phrase that all Muslims say before starting an action. A smooth silence took place for a few minutes as I began my speech. In a quick glance, I scanned the room spotting the potential troublemakers. I looked directly to those few students sitting in the corners and said to them: "I am proud of you brothers," then turned my eyes to the other corner where the naughty girls were sitting and said again "I am proud of you sisters," and ended that strong forward eye contact asking them: "Do you know why am proud of you?"

The whole room echoed: "Why?" I answered, explaining to them how I related to all the students sitting in the room, as originally I had come from the same village. I continued: "You might not recognise me as I am ten years older than you all, but I can still remember some of you as the babies I carried and the kids I played football with in the village desert yards. My name is Ali Abdulkarim Ali Sanqour bin Salim Alsaloom."

As I ended with the words of my full name, an incredible thing happened – the whole room started cheering, clapping and some were just screaming my name as if I had just won a Nobel Prize! By stating my full name and my family nickname, which is very well-known in my village, "Bani yas", I had made an impact and gained the respect of the young students in the room.

That was just the beginning of establishing the respect factor between me and my audience. By enhancing a positive communication base between the students and myself, based on the mutual backgrounds coupled with the respect that I have given them when I said: "I'm so proud of you all brothers and sisters to choose not to give up. To choose to continue to learn and help your country to be more developed and successful, and I'm even more proud because I'm one of you. I come from the same village as you all. How honoured I am to be standing in front of you today."

It was only my voice that could be heard in the room until the very end of my presentation. Students were calm. They listened to every word, piece of advice and story I shared with them. They were willing to listen again and with complete full attention. They continued to show good manners and discipline towards the rest of the invited presenters.

From that day onwards, I have learned more and more about how respect can lead to better communication and understanding and how it all depends on us and our attitude to bridge friendly and honourable relations enriched and powered by respect.

Ali finished his letter to me by saying: "Wealth is not money; wealth is a higher value than what is materialistic. It is your rich soul that is filled with strong belief in your faith, leaders and country. All of which can be gained through one thing – respect."

I truly believe that Ali is a very wealthy individual in more ways than money. He certainly has all the trappings of wealth yet coupled with the qualities he listed above, he has humility and integrity, honour and, of course, the respect that accompanies a man of character.

You can find out more about Ali at: **http://www.ask-ali.com/main.asp.**

Do you think this scenario could be applied to schools around the world? I am pretty certain it could. I know as someone who speaks to students that gaining the respect of a young audience from the outset is essential to the success of the delivery.

What has caused the breakdown of respect for teachers? Is it, as Ali suggests, to do with how we communicate?

- How do you build rapport with your students?

- Is there an atmosphere of mutual respect?

- Do you have problems with student behaviour?

- Do the parents respect the school and staff and vice-versa?

Research suggests that students learn best in a climate of respect for who they are as individuals and respect for what they need as learners. If the concern is about behavioural problems in schools, it has to focus on the general atmosphere of respect in the school and the community that the school serves. If a school expects respect from the students, it has to return that respect.

According to well-known head teacher, Sir Alan Steer: "80% of low-level disruption arises from issues of teaching and management." A vital factor is the quality of teaching. Lessons have to be fast-paced otherwise the students become bored and that can lead to disrespectful behaviour. However, I think we must beware of instant solutions or quick fixes.

It is impossible in just one chapter to deal with the complex issues that surround respect. You may enjoy reading comments on these useful links:

http://news.bbc.co.uk/1/hi/education

http://school.familyeducation.com/parents-and-school/parents-and-teacher

Google and the other search engines will also lead you to international articles on respect, which support Ali's original viewpoint. This would imply that respect or lack of is a global school issue even in counties where respect is a core cultural belief.

Notes: _____

_____

_____

_____

_____

_____

_____

_____

_____

_____

_____

_____

_____

_____

_____

_____

_____

_____

_____

_____

_____

_____

_____

_____

_____

_____

Chapter 9

Thorny issues

surrounding the teaching profession

. . . .

In 2007, Baroness Blackstone stated in the House of Lords: "We have to allow the working group led by the local authority employers to see whether it is possible to remove grossly incompetent teachers. After all, they are damaging the education of children."

How do you feel about Baroness Blackstone's comment? Has she identified a major moral issue? Does her statement generate an emotional response from you? Do you basically agree or disagree? Perhaps society gets the teachers it creates and deserves? In my opinion, educational institutions are microcosms of the culture and the society that supports them. As such, they should be bastions of moral behaviour. Our institutions should be the training ground for staff and students to determine and practise their personal ethics code, which will guide them for the remainder of their lives and professional careers.

As I see it, decisions which have substantial impact are made within administrative bodies. These decisions affect the entire institution, including staff, support personnel, students and even visitors to the school. As such they should be bastions of moral values and should serve as an example for the school community. Higher education has the role of providing not just such examples for students, but of providing students with education in ethical values, including the underlying concepts, critical thinking skills to help in decision making, a broad view of universal ethical codes and a sense of responsibility for others when making personal choices. A quote from the Ethics Workbook (1999) states: "Ethics, like the gyroscope, is a mechanism that must be used consciously and continuously to maintain direction, stability, and equilibrium."

The tragedy is that teachers are often afraid to take ownership of their beliefs. They fear alienation and rebuke as society is all too keen to blame teachers when things go wrong. Faith schools still have a strong underlying ethos of moral guidance and many parents and students are drawn to these educational establishments, yet these too are under government scrutiny.

So it is little wonder that teachers feel disconnected and dissatisfied and go on to consider alternative employment.

Why do teachers leave the profession? One comment from an ex-teacher, Anne, was: "I left due to lack of self development and lack of respect from society." I think this is a common complaint and genuine cause for concern.

If you consider yourself to be a great or outstanding teacher and this is recognised by Ofsted and your peers alike then you should reap the benefits of your dedication and commitment. The government should and could reward you; apart from any financial remuneration, would a fantastic recognition of your abilities not be to reduce your administration load? The amount of paperwork is mind numbing.

Why not enter your comments on the *Love your life...* blog: http://loveyourlife-eilidh.blogspot.com? Together we can campaign to reduce the amount of tedious, repetitive bureaucracy.

I often ask teachers about the issues that concern them most.

Many of these issues were highlighted in a survey I commissioned with teachers and senior leaders in north-west England in 2007.

Overleaf you will find a double page of callouts, why not tick the ones which are relevant to you?

Teachers ask...

Do people ever take me seriously?

Why don't I have enough time?

Am I valued?

Does anybody appreciate what I do?

Why can't I work for a local education authority that thinks about its teachers?

Why do we have so many meetings?

Why don't I get paid more?

Where is classroom discipline?

Why don't they listen?

Do my opinions count?

Why do I have to cover for other people's incompetence?

Where is the respect?

Why do I feel guilty about being off work with stress?

Am I the only one committed to this job?

How do I deal with the bullies?

Why does my department not have enough money?

Could I please have recognition of work well done?

Management ask...

Who reads these league tables?

Why do schools not meet their targets?

Are they just counting the days to retirement?

Why don't they get their lesson plans in on time?

How do you help staff who are facing personal meltdown?

How do you get staff to work collaboratively?

Why do they just defend their own interests?

Where do you find competent senior staff?

Do they recognise that a problem exists?

Do they want
a teaching career?

Do they want
to solve the
problem?

What does
a good head teacher
actually do?

How
do I avoid career
burnout?

How do you
help staff with
personal problems?

How do I give staff
the opportunity to
do what they do
best every day?

Why am I
constantly tired?

So what is the Ofsted
inspection really like?

How do
you build
self-esteem?

Senior managers and leaders have the task of delivering government initiatives. They are often given mixed messages and have the challenge of delivering to the demands of governing bodies, staff, parents and students – as well as the government. There are so many stakeholders to please that a difficult compromise often evolves.

Good teachers want to teach and to be trusted to get on with the job they are trained to do. They play an important role in assisting students to view choices, both professional and personal, as a vital part of their future lives. Therefore we need to encourage and support teachers in their endeavours and teachers need to work on their own self-image and self-belief to gain the recognition they deserve.

Gallup interviewed over a million workers and asked them hundreds of questions. Their report (2001) was the result of over 20 years of testing and was based on 12 key questions that measure workplace satisfaction. As you read these questions opposite, consider whether you feel that they are areas in which you could make a difference and that you could focus on.

Notes:

Measuring workplace satisfaction

1. Do I know what is expected of me at work?

_____

2. Do I have the materials and equipment I need to do my work right?

_____

3. At work, do I have the opportunity to do what I do best every day?

_____

4. In the past seven days, have I received recognition or praise for good work?

_____

5. Does my supervisor seem to care about me as a person?

_____

6. Is there someone at work who encourages my development?

_____

7. Do my opinions seem to count?

_____

8. Am I made to feel that my work is important?

_____

9. Are my co-workers committed to doing quality work?

_____

10. Do I have a best friend at work?

_____

11. In the past six months, have I talked with someone about my progress?

_____

12. At work, have I had opportunities to learn and grow?

This information is particularly useful to school leaders. While they have only limited powers to remunerate, they do have plenty of opportunities to make their colleagues' working lives more pleasant. The Gallup organisation's 25-year-long investigation into what makes a strong workplace found the answer to be one in which people are content and effective.

Abraham Maslow developed a theory called 'The Hierarchy of Needs' in the US in the 1940s, and it remains valid today for understanding human motivation, management training and personal development. His theory states that our first needs are basic biological needs, such as food and shelter to stay alive. Once these have been fulfilled, our next concern is safety. Notice that safety does not have to do with danger; safety needs are actual feelings of comfort and knowing that we are in control of our actions and destiny. The next level consists of psychological needs. First is the need to belong, the second is esteem. Esteem, in addition to belonging, requires that people like and respect you. Sometimes referred to as the highest level, self-actualisation is when you have satisfied all of these other requirements and are then able to develop strong beliefs, values, morals and ethics.

This chapter has posed many questions and offers few concrete solutions. Instead, it encourages careful reflection. One option is to take control of your own personal situation. For this you need self-discipline and to assist you I have included an excerpt from a master practitioner in positive thought. Napoleon Hill was born in 1883 and had a successful career in writing, teaching and lecturing about the principles of success. His work stands as a monument to individual achievement and is the cornerstone of modern motivation. This is his *Creed for Self-Discipline* from his book, *The Master-Key to Riches*:

Willpower:

Recognising that the power of will is the Supreme Court over all other departments of my mind, I will exercise it daily, when I need the urge to action for any purpose; and I will form habits designed to bring the power of my will into action at least once daily.

Emotions:

Realising that my emotions are both positive and negative I will form daily habits which will encourage the development of the positive emotions, and aid me in converting the negative emotions into some form of useful action.

Reason:

Recognising that both my positive emotions and my negative emotions may be dangerous if they are not controlled and guided to desirable ends, I will submit all my desires, aims and purposes to my faculty of reason, and I will be guided by it in giving expression to these.

Imagination:

Recognising the need for sound plans and ideas for the attainment of my desires, I will develop my imagination by calling upon it daily for help in the formation of my plans.

Conscience:

Recognising that my emotions often err in their over-enthusiasm, and my faculty of reason often is without the warmth of feeling that is necessary to enable me to combine justice with mercy in my judgments, I will encourage my conscience to guide me as to what is right and what is wrong, but I will never set aside the verdicts it renders, no matter what may be the cost of carrying them out.

Memory:

Recognising the value of an alert memory, I will encourage mine to become alert by taking care to impress it clearly with all thoughts I wish to recall, and by associating those thoughts with related subjects which I may call to mind frequently.

Subconscious Mind:

Recognising the influence of my subconscious mind over my power of will, I shall take care to submit to it a clear and definite picture of my major purpose in life and all minor purposes leading to my major purpose, and I shall keep this picture constantly before my subconscious mind by repeating it daily.

Signed: _____ Dated: _____

By signing this creed you are taking another positive step in your life plan.

If you wish to download this creed, visit the website and sign up as a member with the code 'LYLmemg88'.

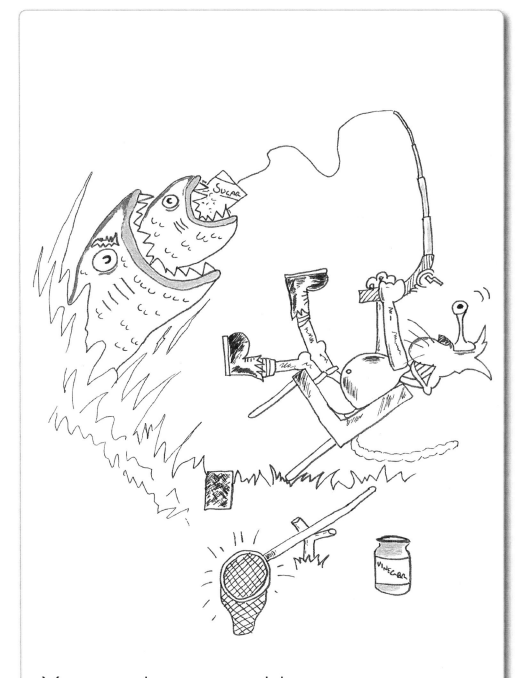

You catch more with
sugar than vinegar

Chapter 10

How to achieve a more balanced work schedule

"The future is something which everyone reaches at the rate of 60 minutes an hour, whatever he does, whoever he is." *CS Lewis, author.*

This chapter includes some simple time management techniques that have been devised and developed to work for education establishments.

Story time

A professor stood before his philosophy class and had some items in front of him. When the class began, he wordlessly picked up a very large and empty mayonnaise jar and proceeded to fill it with golf balls. He then asked the students if the jar was full. They agreed that it was. The professor then picked up a box of pebbles and poured them into the jar.

He shook the jar lightly. The pebbles rolled into the open areas between the golf balls. He then asked the students again if the jar was full. They agreed it was.

The professor next picked up a box of sand and poured it into the jar. Of course, the sand filled up everything else. He asked once more if the jar was full. The students responded with a unanimous "yes."

The professor then produced two beers from under the table and poured the entire contents into the jar effectively filling the empty space between the sand. The students laughed.

"Now," said the professor as the laughter subsided, "I want you to recognise that this jar represents your life. The golf balls are the important things – your family, your children, your health,

*your friends and your favourite passions – and if everything else
was lost and only they remained, your life would still be full. The
pebbles are the other things that matter like your job, your house
and your car. The sand is everything else, the small stuff. If you put
the sand into the jar first," he continued, "there is no room for the
pebbles or the golf balls.*

*"The same goes for life. If you spend all your time and energy
on the small stuff you will never have room for the things that are
important to you. Pay attention to the things that are critical to
your happiness. Play with your children. Take time to get medical
checkups. Take your spouse out to dinner. Play another 18 holes
of golf. There will always be time to clean the house and fix the
waste disposal. Take care of the golf balls first, the things that
really matter. Set your priorities. The rest is just sand."*

*One of the students raised her hand and inquired what the beers
represented. The professor smiled.*

*"I'm glad you asked," the professor said, "It just goes to show
you that no matter how full your life may seem, there's always time
for a couple of beers with a friend."*

I have amended this story slightly and sadly cannot give credit
to the writer as it came in on an email some years ago. I filed
it at that time as I thought it aptly illustrated the importance of
managing time and living a balanced life.

Notes: _____

_____

_____

_____

_____

_____

Top 10 time wasters

What is your number one time waster? We all use the 24 hours we have at our disposal. Sometimes we are more effective than others. Research shows that these are the most common reasons that people waste time:

1. Losing (misplacing) things
2. Meetings
3. The telephone
4. Interruptions
5. Procrastination
6. Task hopping
7. Fire fighting
8. Reverse delegation
9. Perfectionism
10. Distractions

Eilidh's eight time management tips

1. "No" is your most powerful time management tool.
When we know what our values are, and when we have a clear set of goals in all areas of our lives, we are in a much stronger position to politely and appropriately say "no" to potential time-stealers and less relevant activities. When someone asks you to take on another job show them your current list of priorities (have a prepared list of things to do – ten is a good number) and kindly ask them which one they wish you to drop in order to fit in their request.

2. Every week, block in a few important non-urgent actions.
It's too easy to get caught up in everlasting deadlines. To change that emphasis make appointments with yourself, written into your diary or organiser, to work on one or two activities per week of long-lasting value. If you're not sure what sort of things you could be working on, think of the big tasks you're putting off until you have time. Almost certainly they can be broken down into small chunks and there will be something you can start on.

3. Constantly ask: "What is my highest priority right now?"

This is a great focusing question. When we use it as a constant background mantra or self-question we find it easier to stay on task with the activities that really will make a difference. We're also less likely at the end of the day to find we've not dealt with our highest priorities of the day.

4. How can I do this task more efficiently?

Become what I call a "walking question mark". There are always better ways to do things. Every time you do a task, look for a shortcut; look for some way to trim a few seconds or a minute or two off the task. They mount up to a surprising total over the weeks and months.

5. Block in regular sanity gaps.

What point is there in being wonderfully efficient if we don't take time to enjoy our wonderful life and the amazing world we live in? When did you last take a complete weekend off – no email, no business calls and no responsibilities other than the people you're with?

6. Manage your energy well and time looks after itself.

If something isn't flowing smoothly there is almost always an opportunity to either change activity or invest more energy into improving things. If you find yourself saying "I'm tired" on a frequent basis then good filter questions are: "What's blocking my energy here and what can I do about it?"

If your issue is not having time to get to the gym or take regular exercise, then start by running up and down stairs! Unless you are on one level living this is a great way to start. If you are doing a sedentary task such as marking or computer work then keep an eye to the time. Every 45-60 minutes take a break and run up and down stairs, start with five and aim for ten repeat runs. This should get your heart pumping! (Please, however, consider your own health and safety.)

7. Eliminate clutter in all areas of your life.

Not a Man for All Seasons but an Action for All Seasons – have a spring clean! Read my April 2008 Newsletter for more tips and ideas (@).

This way you are much less likely to lose important things in the future and if you are like me you will probably find things you have been hunting for for ages! Have a sort out and you will save time and be tidier. For example:

a) Keys – keep car and house keys on separate key rings and keep in a safe place.

b) Reorganise the office – schedule declutter sessions on a regular basis.

c) Recycle – Clear out your wardrobe and recycle unwanted items to a good cause. You could use **http://www.freecycle.org** or check if there is a Furniture Mine organisation in your area. Reusable items can be refurbished giving training opportunities and also providing appliances and furniture to those on low incomes. Contact: **admin@furnituremine.org.uk** for more information.

8. Don't make email the first thing of the day – unless it suits you.

If you get hooked into email first thing in the day it can take over. In fact, it's an addictive medium. Instead, you take control of your day. Spend time on the most important tasks for the day and, unless it's truly vital that you include an email check first thing, don't come to email until at least mid-morning, and then only for a defined chunk of time. Have two or three email slots through the day and you'll keep on top of most of it. Every now and then you may need a catch up but, in truth, if people are relying on email as the medium for urgent information they're using it wrongly.

A phone is still almost always the best way to alert someone that there's something urgent waiting. The thing is, communication is only what's received, not what is sent. How do you know someone has read your urgent epistle unless you've spoken to them?

Take Time Poem

Take time to THINK... It is the source of power

Take time to PLAY... It is the secret of perpetual youth

Take time to READ... It is the fountain of wisdom

Take time to PRAY... It is the greatest power on earth

Take time to LOVE and BE LOVED... It is a God-given privilege

Take time to BE FRIENDLY... It is the road to happiness

Take time to LAUGH... It is the music of the soul

Take time to GIVE... It is too short a day to be selfish

Take time to WORK... It is the price of success

Take time to DO CHARITY... It is a key to heaven

This anonymous poem was given to me by Mrs Hilda Drury, head teacher.

Time saving tips for administrators

Does your precious teaching and/or administration time seem to be shrinking? Are there never enough hours in the day? Well here is a quick dip of tried and tested practical tips for administrators.

Target the following tasks:

- Declutter
- Reduce interruptions
- Enjoy your own family after a hard day at school
- Simplify and reduce meetings
- Get information back from others on time.

For many years I've been working in schools and colleges. I have also assisted associations, industry groups, professional bodies, local government and voluntary groups. There is a common complaint: "No-one returns our forms – and if they do they are seldom on time!"

From a school view point, there are many ways to get the message out to parents. However, sometimes the children don't pass them on. Sometimes they are lost or just end up in a pile of paperwork in the kitchen.

I would like to encourage schools to match their distribution and receipt methodology to the personality preferences of the families. Some families prefer email; some parents want to collect letters from school; and some prefer post. Whatever you do, put in steps to cover all the options so that one way or another forms will be returned quickly and efficiently. Check at the beginning of each school year that parents want to stay with the same method of communication. Email is not only an easier and cheaper method for a school it is environmentally aware as well.

Examples of best practice:

1. Encourage reward systems so that children take responsibility for returning the forms the next day. An end of term tally, marbles in a jar, smiley faces, a personal letter from the head teacher – the list is endless.

2. In your weekly newsletter mention the letter with its due date. Replies then become as important as the actual date.

It is also a further reminder in case people did not receive the original notice. Regularly inform parents of all the options and encourage them to select what works best for them. Circumstances change and so do attitudes. Information is key.

3. Use school websites as a resource. Upload newsletters and archive old ones. Make forms available to download.

4. Offer the opportunity to have essential information sent to a work email – if appropriate.

5. Start with good habits. In reception, give gentle encouragement in person to people who forget.

6. Keep the format the same across the school, eg correspondence wallet, a notebook for each child, a school diary or planner – something that is completed as part of a constant record.

7. Send out newsletters on a set day of the week. Use brightly coloured paper, possibly rotating the shades.

8. Be understanding yet firm with late payment. A cash payment at the beginning of the year, from which funds are deducted each time a reply is returned, will save the effort of constantly collecting, counting and processing payment. When the figure is down to £5 request the next instalment. End of year balances can either be donated to school funds/school, nominated to charity or returned to the family.

Notes: _____

_____

_____

_____

_____

_____

_____

_____

Plan ahead

- Take time to discuss at length goals and objectives with colleagues/family/team players/coaches/mentors. This is the most crucial stage. It cannot be omitted or abbreviated. Preparation and planning promises perfect performance.

- Learn to say no politely and in a qualified manner. Know when to delegate and when to volunteer.

- Review team plans, confer, discuss and learn to compromise if necessary.

- Buddy up for support or find a mentor/coach.

- If using a to-do list, consider:

Priority	Date	Task	Complete	Not complete	Re-prioritise or delete?

- Mark activities according to low, medium and high priority.

Legend:

*   low priority

**   medium priority

*** high priority

Years ago I was attending a personal development conference as a delegate. I can still remember two key points:

1. Do it now. If a task takes two minutes or less then do it straight away. Get it done and out of the way and feel success. If the task takes longer than a couple of minutes, it must be prioritised and added to the to do list.

2. Don't put it down, put it away! This is a great maxim for a home and office.

Lifestyle assessment

"Either you run the day... or the day runs you." *Jim Rohn (business philosopher).*

	Hours in your day	(hrs per wk)
Work/studies		
Full time/part time one		
Part time two/ Part time three/ Marking/lesson prep		
Voluntary/student/ other		
Home		
Personal grooming time		
With partner		
Child care/parenting		
Cooking		
Shopping		
Cleaning/cars/DIY		
Chauffeuring/driving/ car maintenance		
Domestic chores eg laundry/ dishwasher/kitchen		
Home office/computer		
Add daily % for regular activities		
Sports/gym/walking/craft/DIY/ garden/studies		
Other eg cinema/music/church		

24 hours less sleep allocation = your available daily hours:

Minus hours allocated =

Result =

We all have 24 hours a day and 168 hours per week at our disposal.

Some teachers find it easier to work this chart on a weekly rather than a daily basis. The choice is yours so long as you can identify where you manage your time well and areas for concern.

🕐 Personal action points to consider should be noted below. It is a good idea to date this exercise and review it every month for three months. Note on your calendar a major annual review to chart your progress. Use the calendar on your computer or mobile phone to flag up all such activities as well as noting them in your diary and wall planner.

Notes: _____

_____

_____

_____

_____

_____

_____

_____

_____

_____

_____

_____

_____

_____

_____

_____

_____

_____

_____

The rewards of good time management

1. More time to do what you want to do

2. Satisfaction of a job well done

3. Less stress

4. More control over your own life

5. When a fastball (or life attack) comes upon you, you are in a position of strength to deal with it more effectively.

🕐 Set suitable rewards for yourself as you progress through your goals.

Activity: In order to benefit from all these rewards it is essential to develop the necessary disciplines and habits.

Discuss your roles and responsibilities within the class/year group/school/family or team, for example within your school, what are the responsibilities of the following:

- The site manager
- The teaching assistant
- The school secretary
- Administration and support staff
- Teaching staff
- Senior management
- The head teacher/principal
- Bursar
- PTA or school association members
- Parents/helpers/volunteers
- Senior students (pupils)
- Governors.

Have you ever considered what it is that these people do and how their job relates to yours? If not, take time to consider these matters. It is vital that we all understand the pieces of the jigsaw. The key people should all be given credit in the staff handbook.

❏ This could be a good staff meeting agenda item to start a school term.

Action plan focus

The table below allows you to schedule your top ten priorities in terms of work/life balance.

Date	Task	Mon.	Tues.	Wed.	Thur.	Fri.
	1. Planning					
	2. Lesson preparation					
	3. Teaching					
	4. Meetings					
	5. Marking/admin					
	6. Reading					
	7. Personal time					
	8. Meal time					
	9. Fun/relaxation					
	10. Family time					
Total						

If you monitor your results, note successes and how and where you spend your time, you will find that your available time will grow.

- -

"Growth is not steady, forward, upward progression. It is instead a switchback trail; three steps forward, two back, one around the bushes, and a few simply standing, before another forward leap."

Dorothy Corkille Briggs (teacher, author and school psychologist).

- -

"No-one has ever gone blind from looking at the bright side of life"

(Excerpt from the Cool Beans Desktop)

Chapter 11

How to increase confidence and feel better about yourself

Seven strategies for handling worries

When I deliver my programme on how to deal with difficult people and situations I talk about contingency planning. If you are plagued by a fear or worry why not take a similar approach. Talk yourself through "what if" scenarios and create positive statements for each worry. Each statement should be:

1. In the present tense
2. Do-able
3. Believable
4. Clear and exact
5. Framed positively
6. Something you can change about yourself (not others)
7. Something you believe you deserve.

For example, if you have an interview your positive thinking could be along these lines:

- I am glad I have an interview
- It allows me an opportunity to promote my skills and abilities
- I believe that I can do a first class job
- I have planned and prepared for this moment and know that I am ready for fresh challenges
- I have selected my interview clothes and have them ready with the necessary documents in my briefcase
- I deserve this interview, I am going to enjoy it and give it my best. Interviews are fun!

This mental preparation can be used in many situations such as a driving test, an exam, or a meeting with a difficult parent. This approach will have a dramatic effect on your self-belief and self confidence.

Instant confidence boosters

How you are perceived

If you are smiling, with a direct gaze, erect posture, nodding and leaning forward you will be seen as happy, confident and at ease with nothing to hide. A good stance implies high self-esteem, while leaning into a conversation says that you are interested in what is being said. When you nod it shows approval of the other person's opinion. If you add to these open, as opposed to closed, gestures – the most common closed gesture is folded arms across the body – you will convey an open and honest character. Putting your head to one side says that you are listening positively and with interest.

All of these simple actions are techniques that can be mastered. Make an effort to do so as they will truly increase your confidence.

Increase your visibility

1. Raise your profile. Be well prepared and plan. This will create a positive and professional impact. Your image is very important and extends to your CV or résumé. If necessary seek the advice of an image and style consultant (contact Impression Management Unlimited **www.imu.org.uk**).

2. Be well informed and knowledgeable. Know about your organisation, about your role, function and specialism. Speak up when your topic area is being discussed and offer guidance and support to colleagues.

3. Volunteer. There is nothing better than volunteering your assistance to get you noticed. Offer to organise an event, deliver a report or make a speech at a retirement or leaving party.

4. Prepare short weekly reports. Offer to prepare short reports to your team leader or head of department. Organise tasks with your name on them while you are away. Plan to be seen during long periods of leave such as maternity or sabbatical. This is important if you want to maintain your credibility and standing.

5. Learn the skills of effective networking. Join appropriate associations and support groups and learn to build relationships – these are the glue that will make it all work. Remember, good manners are powerful, especially in this day of electronic communication, so be known for writing thank you notes and letters of appreciation.

6. Carry a business card. Make it easy for people to contact you and ensure you always have a supply of professional crafted cards. Fund yourself if necessary and buy the best you can afford. Remember, the card creates a long lasting impression so think about what you want it to say about you.

7. Have a professional set of photographs taken. This is essential when looking for recognition and promotion. Remember to have them updated regularly.

8. Make memorable presentations. This can be regarded as on-the-job training. You do not get a second chance to make a first impression. Seek a presentation skills course if required (**www.activepresence.co.uk**). Children can be very astute in such matters so practise on them. Ask them for feedback and be prepared to act on it. Think of the benefits to your students – they deserve the best and so do you.

9. Approach the recruiters and be proactive. If you are looking for a new post or a fresh career then find the best agencies both on- and off-line.

10. Mix with the movers and shakers. Choose to mix with influential people. There is always a system within any organisation or business, so learn to work it and, whatever needs to be done, just do it... even better, do it today!

Have an outer body experience

As a teacher, you have a great imagination – it is a prerequisite for the job. So, since you have been imagining, let's consider another little exercise.

Stop what you are currently doing and imagine yourself with the ability to leave your body where it is and put your mind in the top right hand corner of the room you are sitting in. Now look down on yourself from your vantage point, what do you see?

If you were to advise the person you can see to make some changes what would they be? How can they improve their efficiency? Review their lifestyle. Study their results. What is the state of their health and general wellbeing? What are their stress levels? Now move back into your body and ask yourself: if you know this why do you not do it?

Millionaire mentality

"Excellence is not a skill. It is an attitude." *Ralph Marston, Australian Scientist.*

If we cannot all be millionaires (nor have any desire to be so) at least we can have an excellent attitude.

Millionaires and successful wealthy people behave differently in many ways. Here are three things that make them really stand out:

1. They think differently. Normal thinking tends to focus on the negative, ie: "That won't work," or "That can't be done". Millionaires tend to think: "That will work," or "That can be done. I just have to figure out how to do it."

2. They act differently – most people do not act at all on their thoughts and ideas; or only act in a half-hearted fashion and that is destined for failure. Millionaires take positive and enthusiastic action and they fully expect to succeed.

3. They persist. Most people give up at the first hurdle; seeing it as a confirmation of their expectation to fail. If you expect to fail, why bother to get over the hurdles? Millionaires see each hurdle for what it is: one more stepping stone on the road to success. A wealthy person knows – and expects – that setbacks will occur and is mentally prepared to work through them, making changes where necessary and working steadily towards their goals and objectives.

It is the three stages of thinking, acting and persisting, which separate the winners from the losers. If you make use of this process, success is assured. Deviate from the normal style and behaviour patterns. Watch the crowds and avoid whatever they are doing and in many cases do the opposite.

Make sure you travel through life with a first class attitude towards yourself. See yourself like a million dollar package. Let me reiterate the three main points:

1. Think differently – if you keep doing the same things you are going to get the same results

2. Act differently and so change your actions

3. Keep on keeping on! Persistence is a key factor.

As Thomas Jefferson, US president, said: "Nothing can stop the man with the right mental attitude from achieving his goal; nothing on earth can help the man with the wrong mental attitude."

And finally, consider the words of Og Mandino (writer and editor):"My days of whining and complaining about others have come to an end. Nothing is easier than fault finding. All it will do is discolour my personality so that no-one will want to associate with me. That was my old life. No more."

Notes: _____

_____

_____

_____

_____

_____

_____

_____

_____

_____

_____

_____

_____

_____

_____

_____

"Money is just a tool... learn to be a craftsman... always aim to have more money that month."

(Excerpt from the Cool Beans Desktop)

Chapter 12

Is it all worthwhile?
Insights into successful retirement/life planning

It pays "to start with the end in mind", said Stephen Covey in his book, *The Seven Habits of Highly Effective People*. Your retirement or life plan is no different.

Some teachers and leaders are so driven by their day-to-day job that they are not focusing any of their energies into planning for their futures, health and wealth. Does that sound like you? In that case it is time to seriously delegate.

Retirement versus 'stop this job'

"I don't believe in aging. I believe in forever altering one's aspect to the sun." *Virginia Woolf, author.*

It pays to have your own personal life compass. I endorse the sentiments of Virginia Woolf and could easily adopt hers. In the early decades of your life, your main objective is to study and qualify to secure a full time job with a pension. These are your learning years. By your late 30s and 40s you reach your earning years when you can maximise on your savings. The next decades are your yearning years; those are the 60s and beyond when you may find yourself saying: "I wish I had done that... "

Something that you need to do now, if you have not already done so, is write your will. You know it makes sense. So just get it done. You do not want to die intestate. Visit a lawyer or start by doing some research at **http://wisewills.co.uk/intestate.htm**.

Avoid the trap of waiting until the time is right to do important things. Will-writing aside, this list of things to do includes planning when you want your teaching career to end. Have you spent more time planning your annual holidays, projects and landmark birthday parties than you have done planning your future? In terms of having a happy and purposeful retirement with adequate funds and good health, planning is essential. Put time aside to create your own life plan. It is very empowering and within it you need to include a target monetary figure. If you are under 40 you certainly do not want to depend on the state pension system to take care of your needs after you cease working.

There is life after retirement. And I am going to suggest that you scrub the word retirement and start looking at the decades after you stop your teaching career in a different way. You can have a great life after work, especially if you plan to make it happen. I know of one head teacher who retired and opened a schools' supplies shop; another who took early retirement, paid off all his debts and mortgage and went back to college to study photography; a lady who took early retirement to take care of an aging parent and does supply work; and yet another who is currently taking a world-cruise while she decides what to do with the rest of her life. If you are thinking that retirement is the end, or that it is too far off to concern you now, then you need to make a paradigm shift.

Due to the advances of medical sciences and a better understanding of health issues, not only does a larger proportion of society live to retire, but go on to live much longer as well. The number of those living ten years and more beyond the retirement age of 65 has doubled in the past 60 years.

Gender differences

Surveys show that more than 70% of men rate their work as the most important factor in their lives. In the same study more than 70% of women valued their relationships – the quality of the relationships was a measure of their self-worth.

So when a woman retires little changes. She develops fresh interests around friendships; continues her domestic role, maybe joins a gym, learns to paint, takes up golf, studies or gives her time to charity, church or community work. Women choose activities that favour their interest in people and their ability to interact with them. Women are so used to their diverse roles as mothers, partners, grandmothers, friends, carers, domestic goddesses, social secretaries and career women, that embracing retirement is merely another aspect of their lives. Women do what they have always done – they get on with it – and most women never 'retire' as such.

When men retire it can be totally different. In some cases it can be disastrous. In fact, premature death is not uncommon. Men generally define themselves by their work. In retirement, finding new meaning in life must be a priority for a man. Men see themselves as the breadwinners, often with a group of friends with whom they've interacted at work. When men are working they look in the mirror and know who they are. When men no longer have that identity and no longer have the security of income, they can become introspective and insecure.

If men do not plan, the things they had hoped to do in retirement may not be possible financially or physically. Some get into difficulty with their health and their behaviour (such as alcohol) and, statistically, many who functioned at higher levels may die only three to four years after retirement. Do you know of such cases?

Retirement is perceived as a significant loss in the eyes of many men. It is important that men feel that they can make a valuable contribution after they stop work.

"More than 14% of workers in the UK believe they will never have enough money to retire and 20% expect to have to sell their home to help fund their retirement," said the Prudential in 2007.

Failing to plan is planning to fail
"People with goals succeed because they know where they are going. It's as simple as that." Earl Nightingale, author and motivational speaker, made this powerful statement over 40 years ago, and it is as relevant today as it was then.

The number of teachers retiring from the profession is continuing to soar, but fewer are leaving on ill-health grounds, new figures show. Official estimates released by the Department for Children, Schools and Families show the eighth successive increase in as many years. The number retiring on ill health grounds, however, was down by nearly 30% in a year, although those taking premature retirement had increased substantially. These teachers saw a cut in their pensions.

The figures bear out fears of an emerging top-end staffing crisis as baby boomers reach retirement age: 3,350 people in leadership roles retired in 2007. But not all teachers are retiring on particularly healthy pensions; the average annual benefit was just £11,100.

Act as if self-employed

Why? Because many of you will go on to seek some form of further paid employment and having the attitude of being your own boss is attractive to recruitment agencies and future employers. Successful people acknowledge the importance of a mission statement. The highest achievers in any field view themselves as self-employed. They have the attitude that they run their own business, even if they work for others or are affiliated with a major corporation. Managing a school draws many parallels.

And so leaders develop a sense of mission about their career, taking a proactive approach to create the results they want.

A mission statement is a written or typed paragraph. It is posted so that you can see and remember it with ease. It has specific, measurable outcomes and most importantly it has a deadline.

Step A.

Write down five positive personality characteristics. Things you like about yourself in your career or personal life eg willingness to learn, persistence, creativity, friendliness, sense of humour, honesty, etc.

Step B.

For the items you listed above, describe the way you express each positive characteristic on a regular basis in your career, using the word "by" to begin each phrase. For example, if you listed "willingness to learn", you might expand this to read: "By being committed to ongoing professional development". Or if you wrote "persistence", you might write: "By making sure the job always gets done".

Step C.

Write down five goals you'd like to achieve with a date.

Step D.

Look back over Steps A, B and C and circle the three most important items in each case.

Step E.

Now write a paragraph that will become your personal mission statement. When finished, you will have a paragraph that reads something like:

"My purpose is to express my intelligence, creativity and people skills by continually learning and applying new ideas, by finding solutions to my (or my pupils') problems. I will build a powerful network of contacts to help me. I will find a mentor. I will create such a happy atmosphere in my new life/ in my classroom and the school / that everyone will want to work with me. I will gain recognition and promotion/ new job by ＿＿＿＿＿＿＿＿"

and add a month and year.

Date and sign your mission statement.

Follow the guidelines above by:

1. Posting it where you can review it

2. Committing it to memory

3. Reading and reciting it daily.

Do this and you'll be on a mission. Be prepared to succeed! You are taking a major step in creating the life you want to lead.

"First rule of vacations: Take half as many clothes as you planned, and twice as much money." *Anonymous.*

I think this maxim is equally applicable to retirement. Drop at least half of the baggage you picked up during your teaching career and most definitely aim to have twice as much money as you initially planned for. Happy retirement needs serious funding.

Notes: ＿＿＿＿＿＿＿＿＿＿＿＿＿＿＿＿＿＿＿＿＿＿＿＿＿＿＿＿

_____

_____

_____

_____

_____

_____

_____

_____

Story time

John retired early from teaching due to a heart condition. His wife Maureen worked in a law firm. She retired a few years after John. Maureen became concerned when John became withdrawn and retrospective. He missed his work, the company of his colleagues and the contact with the students. He started to drink too much and he was not fun to be around. Maureen sought professional advice. First of all she arranged a medical to get his health issues in perspective. The positive response from his doctor put his mind at rest. Secondly, Maureen arranged an appointment with an Independent Financial Advisor (IFA) to give them a sound financial footing. Both experts put life into perspective and cheered up John considerably. Next Maureen booked them on a weekend on a narrow boat. This way they both had enough activities to keep them busy and the same time plenty of time to sit one-to-one to plan their future.

The outcome was that they realised what a good life they had. They wanted to give back to the community and decided that to volunteer help with parenting classes was something they would both enjoy. They had two happy children of their own and three grandchildren so they felt suitably qualified to offer assistance.

The reassurance from the IFA supported the idea to plan a worldwide trip. Maureen opted to take computer lessons as an outside interest and John found a renewed enthusiasm for cooking.

"In the long run, we shape our lives, and we shape ourselves. The process never ends until we die. And the choices we make are ultimately our responsibility." *Eleanor Roosevelt (First Lady of the United States from 1933 to 1945).*

Ask yourself some questions:

1. Do you want to retire?

2. What is it you want to retire from – elaborate?

3. When do you want to give up full-time work?

4. Will you consider other forms of employment – expand?

5. Where will you retire? Current home? County? Country?

6. Have you discussed your options with loved ones or close friends?

7. Seek advice from retired colleagues. Find out what works for them

8. What will you do to keep mentally active if you do retire?

9. Are you currently putting effort and energy into the next chapter of you life?

10. Have you walked a time-line? Many of my clients have discovered the value of using time-lines to help put their lives in perspective.

Every life is different – our circumstances vary and so do our preferences. There are no rights and wrongs about what you should or should not do when you retire. What is important is that you start planning what you are going to do before the next chapter of your life begins. Take time now to seriously consider the ten questions above.

Seek the professional advice of a coach if necessary.

"Take a few risks!" Do not subscribe to always taking care! It is liberating, empowering and much better fun to take a few risks... always playing safe can be a dangerous attitude.

(Excerpt from the Cool Beans Desktop)

Chapter 13

Final challenges
The beginning or the end?

One teacher in particular has been instrumental in me writing this book. Her name is Mel Cooper and the book is dedicated to her and all the teachers like her. Mel has had her own share of personal problems – divorce, bringing up four children as a single mother, financial issues, work and a full-time college course. Mel is also a mature student. Her enthusiasm and dedication to her students is a constant inspiration.

Great teachers like Mel love their subject and convey that enthusiasm to students. They care about their pupils and they do feel privileged to teach. They view learning as a verb – a doing word – rather than a noun – a mere naming word. Teaching is not neatly packaged facts, but it is an ongoing process of discovery and enlightenment.

There is much debate as to how to measure good teaching. No one is exactly sure how to define excellence in education, because no one ever finishes the process of becoming a master teacher, just as no one ever finally reaches the goal of becoming a truly educated person or the best possible parent. No single style or formula for good teaching can be passed on. To move from good to great, one really has to work at it. Teaching is demanding, and excellent teaching requires enormous dedication and sacrifice. I encourage you to continue on the process of moving forward from good to great and I wish you a joyful and rewarding journey.

Throughout *Love your life - survive the system* I have been issuing challenges and offering advice to teachers and leaders alike. The dictionary definition of a bellwether is any entity in a given arena that serves to create or influence trends or to presage future happenings. I aim to be a bellwether now and issue my penultimate challenge. The first two-part challenge is for the Government, not teachers.

Government education challenge:

For the next three to five years (period to be agreed) starting after the next General Election, agree to make a commitment to teachers to trust them. Allow teachers to get on with the job they have been trained to do.

Government stop list:

1. No more government initiatives, no more policy changes or revisions, no more interfering with the day-to-day running of schools, no more pointless paper chasing exercises, and no more statistics.

2. Stop the pressure on local authorities to supply data and targets figures, allowing schools more freedom to broaden the curriculum and demonstrate that Every Child Matters, thus ensuring that all our young people and their teachers can enjoy and achieve. I do not believe performance management is management at all. It's a facsimile of management. It is leadership by email or management in absentia. Just as teachers have been reduced to human resources, performance management and key performance indicators (KPIs) are reducing education to numbers and learning into digital bytes.
It is time to stop and let teachers teach.

Government to do list:

1. Support and respect teachers, review salaries and terms and conditions. For the agreed period, be reactive not proactive. Respond to schools that ask for help and leave the rest to do not just a good job but a great one.

2. Support staff to implement the key policies that have been put upon them in the past decade and give them the power to veto the irrelevant ones.

Teachers are only becoming familiar with one set of initiatives when another review or revision is thrust upon them. Take for example this statement reported in the Times Education Supplement: "Children could still get a decent education in classes of 70 or more," schools minister Jim Knight claimed. This kind of ill-considered approach is madness and many staff are quietly going crazy in their classrooms.

Imagine the feeling of relief and euphoria if teachers and management alike could go to work confident that the goal posts will stay in place for an agreed period and the only input from government will be encouragement and a commitment to maintain the status quo.

Ofsted versus HMI

In the 12 years that I was a teacher, I had the pleasure of meeting Her Majesty's Inspectors (HMI) on three occasions. I may be looking back through rose-tinted spectacles; however I do not recall any of my colleagues at that time taking time off with stress due to a pending inspection, or in the case of a head teacher in Scotland, committing suicide. What shift in the inspectorate role has brought about such a tragedy?

I recall the inspectors I met as charismatic characters. One in particular has stayed in my memory. He was bright, interested, engaging and challenging. He seemed genuinely keen to know and excited by my maths lesson. He went off and got us both a cup of tea. Then he returned and watched as I completed the lesson; offering ideas and suggestions. I felt as though we were working together. At the end of the teaching day, there was more tea and offers of support and camaraderie. I felt he was as much my colleague and mentor as my inspector. He was full of praise for my class and my teaching abilities.

Nonetheless, he pointed out areas that could be strengthened and improved upon and he suggested courses that I could attend. The whole experience was rewarding and cheering and most importantly carried out and completed on the same day. I did not have to agonise over pending results, which would be posted on the internet for the entire world to see. I went home jubilant and keen to be even better at my job.

I may be misinformed, but I don't think Ofsted works this way today, does it? I refer you to the interview with PD in Chapter 2: *Why did you start this journey.*

So my second challenge for the government is to initiate a dialogue between the former HMIs, retired head teachers and representatives from the teachers' unions and ask them to review the current Ofsted methods. Ofsted inspectors are also bound by KPIs too and hence the absurd paradox. How can they inspect independently, fairly and objectively when they are bound by bureaucracy as well?

It is not my intention to be unduly critical of the current government position of Ofsted. A quotation from EB White (American writer) comes to mind: "Prejudice is a great time saver. You can form opinions without having to get the facts," and throughout the book I have been discussing balance not bias. It is a fact that all political parties like to get involved in education as it attracts the attention of the voting public. Therefore this challenge is issued to all the political leaders.

Challenge for Eilidh

I will create a facility for teachers, parents and other interested parties to register their support for teachers.

---

http://loveyourlife-eilidh.blogspot.com

If you agree with these challenges register your support on this forum.

If you give me enough ammuniton, I will personally plead the case for teachers in Westminster.

Notes:

Cats don't cry over
spilt milk

Chapter 14

Happiness – one last action point

You would not have children to teach without their parents selecting your school. So, let's leave the last contribution to a mother, Sarah Perris – a parent of 11-year old twins who is very supportive of her school and teachers in general, but not of the current system:

"I would like to see an acknowledgement of children's softer skills in our system – their social and emotional intelligence. Quite simply, there seems to be very little, if any. We are breeding generations of monkeys trained to pass particular tests, which fail them when they go out into the real world.

"But the teaching community must know deep in their hearts that the whole system is often meaningless and that children are being taught strategies for passing exams and missing out on the whole point of education – acquiring knowledge.

"My girls actually come home and tell me what they have been taught on a daily basis and their learning is always focused on what will help them get a higher grade in their year six SATS. How sad is that?

"I want my girls to love learning and soak up knowledge and information like fresh sponges, but all they do is stress over what grades they are going to get in exams that are totally meaningless to them. And they are only 11 years of age! I didn't know the meaning of stress until I started my first job at the age of 20!

"If the SAT results don't seriously influence their high school streaming or anything else, what is the point? Parents often do not understand the system and think that getting good SAT results is vital and so they apply even more pressure. Many parents used to be happy with SAT level three to four at the end of the primary stage. Now they all seem to push for level five. This makes a mockery of the whole process. We cannot all be A-star students. Like most parents (and teachers) all I really want is happy children."

You may take issue with some of Sarah's strong opinions, however consider these following results from a recent study. If we look to the happiness factor in children, according to UNICEF, Britain's children are the unhappiest in the West. This was revealed in 2008 as the result of a study conducted in 21 industrialised countries. Britain languishes at the bottom of the wellbeing league table.

As a result, says Professor Jonathan Bradshaw CBE, one of the authors of *Report Card 7: an Overview of Child Wellbeing in Rich Countries*, Britain is a "picture of neglect". This is a sad indictment on British society.

With my overseas work, it is easy for me to see parallels in the problems encountered in education around the world. There are so many similarities in schools, especially those working within an English-speaking environment. There are common issues wherever I have spoken and coached – stress related matters, wellbeing, lack of recognition and coping with change.

A considerable number of teachers, like the children they teach, do not seem to be very happy with their circumstances. And this has come about within a generation, because although there was dissatisfaction in my era, it was not the general malaise that appears to exist in many UK schools today.

Do you need to take action?

Benjamin Disraeli (statesman and literary figure) said:
"Action may not always bring happiness, but there is no happiness without action."

Are you a happy teacher?

Are you happy with your self-development progress thus far?

As you read the book has it connected with your emotions eg happiness?

Let me reiterate what I said at the end of Chapter 1: we have all learned things about ourselves as we have grown up. In some of the more enlightened moments there have been some really progressive thoughts and actions. So as you are about to start the next chapter of your life and career, I have a key action for you. Here is the final challenge:

What do you want to improve about your situation **right now?**

Write down ONE key point:

1. _____

I commend this challenge to you! I am sure if you embrace it, you will increase your personal happiness factor and that will, in turn, benefit those you teach and work with. James M Barrie (author) said it succinctly: "Those who bring sunshine into the lives of others, cannot keep it from themselves."

Now go forward and take action!

I wish you good health, much happiness, lots of sunshine or as Schweitzer suggests:

"Happiness is nothing more than good health and a bad memory." *Albert Schweitzer (missionary and winner of the Nobel Peace Prize, 1952).*

Notes: _____

_____

_____

_____

_____

_____

_____

_____

_____

_____

Further resources

We can all do with a daily dose of positivity. You might like to have a thought provoking story hit your email box every day. If so, register with: **subscription@mydailyinsights.com** or visit **http://www.nightingaleconant.com** and **http://www.worldofquotes. com** for a free motivational quotation every day.

Here is an example from author and writer William Arthur Ward: "Optimists enrich the present, enhance the future, challenge the improbable and attain the impossible."

If you know of another good source of worthwhile information then please share it with the readership and post a comment on the Blog **http://loveyourlife-eilidh.blogspot.com**.

Thank you!

Linda Brakeall – American author
http://www.lindabrakeall.com

Jan Vermeiren – *Let's Connect*
http://www.janvermeiren.com/

Dr R H Schuller – self-help books
http://en.wikipedia.org/wiki/Robert_H._Schuller

Dr Maxwell Maltz – author
http://www.psycho-cybernetics.com/maltz.html

Professor Jonathan Bradshaw CBE
http://www-users.york.ac.uk/%7Ejrb1/

Comenius Programme:
http://ec.europa.eu/education/programmes/llp/comenius/index_en.html

---

More from Eilidh…

If you want to receive tips and ideas for a happier more balanced life, simply register for the quarterly newsletter on my website.

Bibliography

Albom, M. (2003). *Tuesdays with Morrie: An Old Man, a Young Man and Life's Greatest Lesson*. New York; Time Warner Paperbacks.

Barmby, P. (2006). *Improving teacher recruitment and retention: the importance of workload and pupil behaviour*. Educational Research. 48 (3), pp247-265.

Collins, J. (2001). *Good to Great*. London; Random House Business Books.

Covey, S. (1990). *The Seven Habits of Highly Effective People: Restoring the Character Ethic*. Cambridge; Simon and Schuster.

Emmons, R. and McCullough, M. (2003). *Counting Blessings Versus Burdens: An Experimental Investigation of Gratitude and Subjective Well-Being in Daily Life*. Journal of Personality and Social Psychology. 84 (2), pp 377-389.

Grey, D. (2003). *100 Essential Lists for Teachers*. London; Continuum International Publishing Group.

Hanzak, E. (2005). *Eyes Without Sparkle: A Journey Through Postnatal Illness*. Oxford; Radcliffe Publishing Limited.

Helmstetter, S.(1991) *What to Say When You Talk to Yourself*. London; Thorsons.

Hill, N. (2003). *The Master Key to Riches*. Minnesota, Fawcett Books.

Johnson, S. (1999). *Who Moved My Cheese? An Amazing Way to Deal with Change in Your Work and in Your Life*. London; Vermilion.

Kivimaki, M., Vahtera, J., Elovainio, M. et al (2005). Optimism and Pessimism as Predictors of Change in Health After Death or Onset of Severe Illness in Family. *Health Psychology*. 24(4), pp413-421.

Maslow, A. H. (1943) *A Theory of Human Motivation*. Psychological Review, 50, pp370-396.

McCormack, M. (1994). *What They Don't Teach You at Harvard Business School*. New York; Profile Business.

Milnes, E. (2006). *Cool Beans – The Positive Person's Desktop*. Cheshire; self-published.

National Union of Teachers. (1999) *Tackling Teacher Stress*. London; NUT.

National Union of Teachers. (2007) *Teacher Stress - 2007 Update*. London; NUT.

Seligman, M.E.P. (2002). *Authentic Happiness: Using the New Positive Psychology to Realize Your Potential for Lasting Fulfillment*. New York: Free Press.

Thackray, J. (2001). *Feedback for Real*. Gallup Management Journal 1(1), pp1-5

Tiatorio, A. (1999). *The Ethics Workbook*. Massachusetts; self published.

Vermeiren, J. (2007). *Let's Connect! A Practical Guide for Highly Effective Professional Networking*. New York; Morgan James Publishing.

Webster, A. (2003). *Polar Bear Pirates and Their Quest to Reach Fat City: A Grown Up's Book for Kids at Work*. London; Bantam Books.

Acknowledgements

Sincere thanks to the following for their support and contributions:

Ali Alsaloom	http://www.ask-ali.com/
Carolyn Casserley	
Debbie Catt	http://www.cattconsulting.com/
Mel Cooper	
Val Cotterill	
Sheila Cox	
Chris Davidson	http://www.professionalspeakersjournal.com/
Shirley Davies	
Kath Dennis	
Joy Drew	
Mindy Gibbins-Klein – The Book Midwife	http://www.bookmidwife.com/
Ann Griffiths	
Elaine Hanzak	http://elainehanzak.co.uk/
David Hyner	info@stretchdevelopment.com
Nancy Lake	
Margaret McEwen	
Sue Richardson and the team at Word4Word Publishing	http://www.w4wdp.com/
Geoff Ramm	http://www.mercurymarketing.co.uk/
Chris Roycroft-Davis	http://www.chrisroycroftdavis.com/
Kate Spratley Web Design	http://www.katesprately.com/
Jacqui Ratcliffe	
Mick Waters	
Val Webster	
Philip Whiston	
Phil Wyatt	

Notes:

Notes:

Notes:

Notes: